A CHRISTIAN COSMOLOGY

Volume 3. *A VISION FOR OUR TIMES:*
In the Sadness of the Modern World **(1988)**
Response to the need for a cosmology that incorporates modern
science into a religious view of the world and offers meaning.
Use is made of new concepts of physics (quantum mechanics)
and philosophy (process thought).

Volume 4. *THE LIVING UNIVERSE:*
An Organic Theory of Mind and Matter **(1990)**
An interpretation of quantum mechanics with the synthesis of
Aristotelian and Whiteheadian concepts results in a process
cosmology. The relationship of the cosmos to the transcendent
reality of God.

Volume 5. *CREATION, EVIL, AND THE TRINITY:*
A Christian Process Theology **(1990)**
Integration of the new cosmology into a wider theological
synthesis shows Christian revelation on this process basis to
illuminate the fundamental nature of reality in a fresh way.

Volume 6. *THE MASS ON THE WORLD*
A Modern Theory of Transubstantiation **(2008)**
Reprint in three languages (English, German, and Spanish)
of the author's study concerning the teaching of the Catholic
Church on the real presence of Christ in the Eucharist.

Richard J. Pendergast, SJ
1927–2012

The Mass on the World

A Modern Theory
of Transubstantiation

by

RICHARD J. PENDERGAST, SJ

Edited by
Valerie Miké

A Herder & Herder Book
The Crossroad Publishing Company
New York

A collaboration with The Ethics of Evidence Foundation, Inc.

A Herder & Herder Book
The Crossroad Publishing Company
www.crossroadpublishing.com

Cover design by George Foster after the original of John Miké
Hubble Telescope image of a star formation region in jet HH 901 of the Carina Nebula

Library of Congress Cataloging-in-Publication Data
available from the Library of Congress.

ISBN   cloth   9780824598112
ISBN   ePub   9780824503932 ·
ISBN   mobi   9780824503949
ISBN   Tradepaper   9780824503918

Verum caro, panem verum
verbo carnem efficit,
fitque sanguis Christi merum.

The incarnate Word, by words,
changes real bread into the body
and wine into the blood of Christ.

St. Thomas Aquinas,
PANGE LINGUA

Contents

Foreword: The Eucharist
by Valerie Miké xiii

Original Article
THE MASS ON THE WORLD 1

Article in German
DIE MESSE ÜBER DIE WELT 21

Article in Spanish
LA MISA SOBRE EL MUNDO 45

A New Meaning of Christian Worship
by Pope Benedict XVI 67

About the Author 69

About the Editor 71

FOREWORD

The Eucharist

The real presence of Christ in the Eucharist is the central tenet of Catholicism. A recent study reported that the majority of Catholics no longer hold this belief, and critics point out that the traditional explanation of the Church rests on obsolete science. In this 2008 essay Richard Pendergast offers a modern theory of transubstantiation in the broad context of a historical overview. Given the importance of the subject, we decided to include this reprint in the series of the author's previously unpublished work, with translation in two other languages, German and Spanish.

The Catholic college I attended in the 1950s required four years of coursework in both philosophy and theology. We had the history of philosophy from antiquity to the present and biblical studies, but the predominant theme was the teaching of St. Thomas Aquinas, based on the philosophy of Aristotle. We were introduced to the major principles of Aristotelian metaphysics, their definitions with everyday examples, and studied how they were used to develop theories. The people and things of the world were substances, composed of prime matter, the universal building material, with each substance defined by its own form. The further characteristics of a substance were its accidents. This schema of substance as matter and form (in Greek *hylē* and *morphē*) was called hylomorphism.

The Mass was in Latin. Most students, myself included, had studied Latin, so that participation in the liturgy came naturally. We learned about transubstantiation. When during Mass the priest spoke the words *HOC EST ENIM CORPUS MEUM,* the substance of the bread became the body of Christ, while its accidents remained unchanged. Thus, the appearance and other properties of the bread were still the same, but there was no longer a substance of bread. New to philosophy and eager to understand, I wondered what this theory would mean to me if I did not already believe.

The celebration of First Communion was an important event of my childhood, and I remember strewing rose petals before the Blessed Sacrament from my little basket in a Corpus Christi Day procession along the streets of Budapest. I also recall the solemn beauty of Benedictions in the college chapel, the blessing with the host in the monstrance, as we sang Eucharistic hymns of adoration. Etched sharply in my memory all these years has been a verse from Pange Lingua that says, *Praestet fides supplementum sensuum defectui*, meaning: May faith provide when the senses fail. The fact that these lines were also written by St. Thomas Aquinas was a solace to me at eighteen.

As the article relates, there had in fact been problems with the Aristotelian theory for some time, with the advent of the new physics and the holistic theory of matter, of molecules, atoms, and elementary particles.

When I first read this essay a number of years ago, my immediate reaction was that I would enjoy teaching the new theory. Why? Because it is so intuitive, because its basic structure is already part of the popular consciousness. The author sees the world as a hierarchy of irreducible levels of entities, of increasing complexity and function, from the smallest components of matter, to objects, plants, animals, and human beings. On the highest level is a single entity, the Logos. Entities on the lower levels when integrated into the higher levels retain their own identity. To illustrate this relation of the levels, the article cites the analogy of the five levels of human speech: voice, words, sentences, style, and literary composition.

As a name for raising an entity to a higher level, the author refers to what he calls the original Hegelian term "sublation." Here we need to add an important point of clarification. Hegel introduced the German verb *aufheben* (translated into English as "to sublate") into philosophy, but he did not create it. The word existed in the German language long before him, as it still does today. The present author uses the term to describe his own theory, which is unrelated to Hegelian thought: When during consecration the Eucharistic bread and wine are sublated from their natural level to the highest level of the hierarchy, they are integrated into the incarnate Word with their identity unchanged.

Two bishops who have endorsed the work of Richard Pendergast are listed on the back cover, a Benedictine and a Jesuit, and I had the privilege of extended discussions with both. Bishop Astric Várszegi spoke of historical perspective. Building on the immense treasury of the Church fathers, great believers like St. Benedict in the beginning, St. Thomas in the Middle Ages, and the contemporary Jesuits, with many others along the way, expressed what they saw in the language of their day. The Eucharist is a sign and promise of the final transformation of the world, and Teilhard de Chardin related the image of the host in the monstrance that began to grow and kept expanding as it embraced the universe. It was a vision in our age, but the reality has always been the same.

Valerie Miké
President, The Ethics of Evidence Foundation
June 24, 2020

ORIGINAL ARTICLE

THE MASS ON THE WORLD

I. Eucharistic Theology and Cosmology
II. Transubstantiation
III. The Sacramental Universe
Notes

The Mass on the World

The present article has three sections. The first one discusses the relationship of the theological theory of transubstantiation to that of *transmogrification* (change of meaning) and *transfinalization* (change of finality), ideas that were introduced just before the time of Vatican II by northern European theologians. The second section develops a holistic view of the nature of matter. Our present scientific knowledge seems to require that we abandon the Aristotelian theory of hylomorphism in favor of a theory in which real beings of a certain level "sublate" real but subordinate beings of lower levels. For example, a human being is a substance that includes within itself many smaller substances. When he was in the flesh, the physical body *of* Christ included within itself a vast number of interconnected atoms and molecules. The third section discusses ideas of Teilhard de Chardin about the relationship of Christ to matter.

I. EUCHARISTIC THEOLOGY AND COSMOLOGY

In the sixteenth century the Council of Trent stated the Church's teaching about the Eucharist in a way that seemed to presuppose an Aristotelian-Thomistic conceptual point of view.

> If anyone says that in the holy sacrament of the Eucharist the substance of bread and wine remains together with the body and blood of our Lord Jesus Christ, and denies that wonderful and unique change of the whole substance of the bread into His body and of the whole substance of the wine into His blood while only the species of bread and wine

remain, a change which the Catholic Church very fittingly calls tran-substantiation, *anathema sit.*[1]

The easiest and clearest way to understand this teaching was in terms of the scholastic doctrine of substance and accidents. According to Aristotle, accidents exist in and through substances, qualifying them in various ways. St. Thomas suggested that in the Eucharist we have a unique case in which one substance is changed into another without the accidents of the former one perishing. By the miraculous power of God the accidents of bread and wine remain even after the substance in which they inhered has disappeared. How this could be was, of course, very difficult to see, but then no one expected to be able to understand the Eucharist completely.

However, in fact the decree of the Council of Trent did not use the Aristotelian term "accidents," but instead employed the Latin "species," a more ambiguous term which could mean an objective meaning like "accidents," or a subjective one like "appearances." Whether the species are objective, like Aristotelian accidents, or are more like subjective appearances, is not immediately apparent.

Can we take this as an indication that Trent was cautious and did not wish to endorse Aristotelianism or any other philosophical theory, and that therefore not only "species" but also "substance*" should be interpreted in a very broad general sense? Writing soon after the Second Vatican Council, E. Schillebeeckx stated that this is the opinion of most modern historians of the Council of Trent.[2] However, his own opinion was more complex. In his view, while it is true that Trent did not wish to canonize Aristotelianism, the thinking of the Council Fathers was necessarily bound up with the Aristotelian conceptual system in which most of them were trained. Only by using the categories of Aristotelianism were they able to express their faith in the real presence of Christ in the Eucharist.

In a 1967 article, Schillebeeckx's Dutch colleague Schoonenberg said more or less the same thing: "This shows that the statement of belief made by a council or by anybody else can never be satisfactorily detached from contemporary theological thought, and certainly not by those who themselves made that statement. But we, in a later age, *can* detach the formulation of belief from its historical circumstances."[3]

The distinction between fundamental dogmatic truth and its formulation is shown by the history of the doctrine of the Eucharist previous to Trent. According to Schillebeeckx, three levels can be distinguished in the thirteenth-century teaching of Aquinas on the Eucharist: (1) the level of *faith* in the real presence, (2) the level on which a real *ontological* change in the Eucharistic species is asserted, and (3) the level in which this ontological change is expressed in terms of Aristotelian categories (E 63). Schillebeeckx claimed that today the Aristotelian categories can be seen to be inadequate, and so Aquinas's teaching must be put aside. But what about the ontological level? Belief in an ontological change in the Eucharistic bread and wine goes back to the Greek Fathers of the Church. As Schillebeeckx said, they did not think of substance in Aristotelian terms but in terms of independent being or fundamental reality. The way the Logos takes possession of the Eucharistic elements was, for them, comparable to the way in which he first took possession of his body in the womb of his mother, the Virgin Mary. Both these events came about by the power of the Holy Spirit. Thus, for them, in the Eucharist the bread and wine lost their independent reality, or substance, and became the body and blood of Christ. The fundamental Patristic faith was the same as that of Trent but was expressed in different, non-Aristotelian categories. There is a real ontological change in the Eucharistic elements and it is this change that lends its special character to the Eucharist. There is, then, a basic non-Aristotelian meaning of "substance" in the tradition that led to Trent.

> It was essential and fundamental to the dogma of faith that there should be no *reality* bread after the consecration, since, if the ultimate *reality* present in the Eucharist were to be called bread, there would be simply bread (a reality cannot at the same time be two realities!) and the Eucharistic presence could only be conceived symbolically. . . .
>
> . . . It was only in an attempt to explain the "remaining of the species" that the theory of substance and accidents arose in the minds of the fathers of the Council, with the result that, speaking *traditionally* of

the "substance" of bread, they inevitably produced a contrast between substance and accidents. (E 74–75)

Therefore, even though its Aristotelian formulation can be dispensed with, Trent's understanding of Eucharistic presence not only asserts its reality but also requires an ontological change in the Eucharistic elements, "In other words, the presence of an *ontological aspect* in the *sacramental* giving of the bread is without doubt a datum of faith and not simply an aspect of "wording" (E 81–82). Thus Schillebeeckx concluded that Trent does not have to be interpreted in Aristotelian-Thomistic categories. Nevertheless, he did think that there has to be an ontological change with regard to the Eucharistic elements, just as in the mind of the Church Fathers there had to be an ontological change with regard to the formation of Christ's body in the womb of the Virgin Mary.

The relationship between the Eucharist and cosmological theories remained a problem for Catholic orthodoxy long after Trent. The dominant school of Counter Reformation thought interpreted the basic dogma in terms of the relatively clear (yet at the same time baffling) Aristotelian-Thomistic theory of hylomorphism, and, in an age of violent religious polemics, was not inclined to be tolerant of alternative ones. Thus, in 1663 Descartes's *Meditations* were placed on the Roman Index of Forbidden Books because his understanding of matter was deemed incompatible with Eucharistic doctrine.[4] Our century, of course, is less naive with regard to both theological and scientific theories than the sixteenth. Nor do we demand as much integration between physics and theology as former ages did. Nevertheless, the same basic problem has reappeared again in our own time. Schillebeeckx writes;

> It had already become clear in the period between the two world wars that transubstantiation was in need of reinterpretation. The facts of modern physics had shaken the neo-scholastic speculations about the concept of substance to their foundations. . . .
>
> . . . An almost incalculable number of books and articles concerning the impact of the positive sciences on the traditional understanding of the Eucharist appeared between the two world wars. . . .
>
> . . . Because the theologians who were trying to link the findings of

this new science to the concept of transubstantiation came to conclusions which offered no prospects and because their point of departure was that an ontological change could not leave the physical reality intact, they themselves contributed most of all to the view that an understanding of the Eucharist in terms of natural philosophy was untenable. (E 94–96)

This growing belief was one of the factors that led to the adoption of a different more personalist approach by north European theologians after World War II. Another factor was contemporary developments in philosophy that afforded new categories that seemed better suited for expressing the human and symbolic nature of the sacraments in general and of the Eucharist in particular. Existentialist, phenomenological, and hermeneutical thought does not operate in the ontic mode proper to the sciences, but within a horizon mainly determined by subjective human experience, personal and symbolic self-expression, and interpersonal communication. Within this horizon the action of Christ in the Eucharist is seen in terms of meaning and symbolic self-expression rather than the more objective and cosmological concepts of neo-scholasticism. As a result the change in the Eucharistic elements of bread and wine that takes place at the consecration of the Mass is understood more as a change of meaning and purpose than of substance. Hence the terms "transignification" (change of meaning) and "transfinalization" (change of finality) come to the fore, rather than the traditional "transubstantiation" (change of substance).

However, there are difficulties regarding this anthropological approach. In 1965, Pope Paul VI issued his encyclical *Mysterium Fidei*. Among the opinions with which he took issue was the claim that the change of the meaning of finality of the Eucharistic elements, which is entailed by their role in the symbolic and sacramental action of the Mass, provides an adequate explanation of transubstantiation. In his view the authoritative tradition of the Church demonstrates that there is an ontological change in the consecrated species that goes beyond what can be expressed in terms of meaning and symbolism. The traditional term "transubstantiation" expresses this and cannot be dispensed with in favor of "transignification" or "transfinalization."

Schillebeeckx and Schoonenberg responded in different ways to such critical observations regarding transignification. Commenting on *Mysterium Fidei,* the latter distinguishes between two kinds of action-signs:

> There are action-signs that *bring something to our knowledge,* and so lead to instruction, provoke feelings or transmit a command (for the latter, think of traffic signals). But there are also action-signs and here the *action* is of prime importance—where what is shown forth is at the same time communicated or at least offered. The content of this second kind of action-signs is always a kind of love or communion—shaking hands, a kiss, etc. This second kind fully deserves the designation "effective signs," although the first kind is also effective in some degree in that it communicates knowledge and so also establishes some sort of communion, although only very implicitly. We might therefore speak of "informative" signs on the one hand, and "communicating" signs on the other. (T 88)

According to Schoonenberg, *Mysterium Fidei* had only informative signs in mind when it denied that the transubstantiation of the Eucharistic species can be accounted for in terms of transignification. But the Eucharist is a communicating sign "in which the Lord gives his body in order to make us into his body and in which he gives himself to us for communion in and with him" (T 90).

Schillebeeckx responded differently. While agreeing with Schoonenberg and the English theologian Charles Davis on the importance and utility of the anthropological approach to understanding the Eucharist, he nevertheless asked, "Is transignification identical with transubstantiation, or is it a consequence or an implication of transubstantiation? The question that arises here in its full extent is that of reality" (E 145). His answer was: "Several modern authors correctly regard the creation, the beginning of the covenant of grace, as the background to the eucharistic event as well" (E 127). Reading Church tradition in the light of that principle he could not

> personally be satisfied with a *purely* phenomenological interpretation without metaphysical density. Reality is not man's handiwork—in this sense, realism is essential to the Christian faith. In my reinterpretation

of the Tridentine datum, then, I can never rest content simply with an appeal to a human *giving of meaning alone,* even if this is situated within faith. Of course, a transignification of this kind has a place in the Eucharist, but it is borne up and evoked by the recreative activity of the Holy Spirit, the Spirit of Christ sent by the Father. God himself *acts* in the sphere of the actively believing, doing and celebrating Church, and the result of this divine saving activity is sacramentally a "new creation" which perpetuates and deepens our eschatological relationship to the kingdom of God. (E 150–51)

In saying that "[r]eality is not man's handiwork" Schillebeeckx put his finger on a vital weakness of the attempt to explain the Eucharist completely in terms of transignification. When a young man gives his fiancée a ring, his symbolic action changes the human situation in a very important way.[5] But it does not affect the physical nature of the ring. One might perhaps say that it does change the "relational reality* of the ring, but such a change is not sufficient to express the sense of Church tradition about the Eucharist. The glorified Christ can give himself with a completeness and power that is not possible to ordinary human beings, and, as Schillebeeckx says, his Eucharistic self-giving is a gift of himself, not of himself in a gift (E 138–39). The analogy between human gift giving and Christ's gift of self in the Eucharist is too remote and too weak to have adequate explanatory power.

Schoonenberg is evading the necessity of constructing a cosmology that would take our modern scientific knowledge of matter seriously and would also provide categories in terms of which transubstantiation can be understood. The claim that a material object is transubstantiated purely and simply by assuming a role in a sign-action is too weak. The dissatisfaction expressed in *Mysterium Fidei* is not groundless. Even though Aristotelian-scholastic cosmology is inadequate, the doctrine of transubstantiation continues to express the Church's concern about the reality of matter and the real contribution matter makes to existence even on the spiritual level. If matter is sublimated into ideas, spiritual reality itself will eventually evaporate into wishful thinking and pious desires.

Schillebeeckx's conclusion that transignification is not equivalent to or identical with transubstantiation is undoubtedly correct. However, he does not go very far in explaining the "how" of the Eucharistic presence even though he does insist that it is indeed inseparable from it (E 155–56). In the Middle Ages the problem of the relationship between Eucharistic theology and cosmology was unavoidable, as well as insoluble, in view of the common assumption that the theory of hylomorphism is correct. Now, however, a different theory of matter is available to us. In our age theology cannot avoid taking science into account and, as John Paul II has insisted, we must learn to cope with it.[6] Failure to integrate cosmological considerations into one's theology renders the latter ethereal or idealistic. We simply cannot forget what we know about the structure of matter.

It seems to me that today the state of the question about transubstantiation is essentially the same that Paul VI, Schillebeeckx, and Schoonenberg left us in the 1960s. Theologians have turned their attention to various other aspects of the Eucharist, but the perplexing question raised then still remains. I suppose one reason is because most theologians avoid thinking about scientific questions and most scientists avoid theological ones. But in any event, I turn now to the task of developing a satisfactory modern account of transubstantiation.

II. TRANSUBSTANTIATION

The New Testament employs the term "body" with reference to Christ in at least three somewhat different ways: Jesus is a man and therefore he has a physical body. He is intimately united and identified with the Church and so he also has a mystical body. By eating the Eucharist we eat his body, and thus he has a Eucharistic body, In addition there is probably a fourth body referred to in the New Testament. Teilhard de Chardin found inspiration in several famous passages from St. Paul that speak of the cosmic stature and role of Christ.[7] One of them is Colossians 1:15–20, which is probably an adaptation of an early Christian hymn that praised Christ's lordship over the whole creation. This hymn seems to have claimed that he is the head of the body, meaning, in this context, the cosmic body prominent in Hellenistic thought.[8] In the canonical text of

Colossians the author has changed the reference of "body" to the Church. However, it would seem that this did not change the general understanding in Colossians of the relationship between Christ and the cosmos, which I express here by saying that he has a "cosmic body," to distinguish it from his "mystical body," the Church.

These four bodies of Christ are, of course, closely related, I express this by saying that they are "inadequately distinct." Their distinction does not prevent them from constituting one single reality, for they are aspects of the comprehensive reality of the incarnate Logos. As we shall see, each body exemplifies a common pattern that is verified somewhat differently in each case.

I believe that to understand this, one must first understand what I call "the cosmic hierarchy." Modern natural science has discovered within human beings a hierarchy of smaller entities, namely, organisms, organs and tissues, cells, molecules, atoms, nucleons, electrons and quarks, and is now wondering about even smaller ones. Thus, all entities in the hierarchy (on any but the lowest level) are composed of one or more subordinate ones from levels beneath them.

A crucial question is whether or not a given entity can be "reduced" to the entities within it. Which types of entity can be reduced without remainder to those on lower levels and which ones, if any, cannot? When one says that a particular entity is irreducible, one means that it possesses unique "higher-level" properties that cannot be explained in terms of the subordinate entities within it. Those lower entities contribute to the properties of the higher entity, but the latter has something more. In its action it displays a higher quality—and on the higher levels, a unified consciousness—that can never be explained by the subordinate entities within it. On the other hand, if an entity is reducible, then it can be explained entirely in terms of the lower entities. In this case, the seemingly unified action of the higher entity is entirely due to the interaction of the smaller entities.

In our present theological context we can take for granted that rational entities like ourselves cannot be reduced to lower levels. Indeed, I expect that most readers will agree with my assertion that there are a number of irreducible levels in the natural hierarchy. I believe they include at least the inanimate, animate, sentient, and rational levels, as well as the cosmic level, whose unique entity is the cosmic Christ. In my opinion there is also a lowest, and as yet unknown elementary inanimate level. It is quite possible that there are more, but for our purposes it is sufficient to consider only the six I have mentioned. The entity on a given level has an essential property that none of the lower ones possesses. Thus, neither a rational entity like a human being nor a sentient entity like a dog can be explained completely in terms of its components. The smallest entities of the lowest, inanimate level are, of course, irreducible. They are the "atoms" of the ancient Greeks, out of which everything else is made. I call them "elementary entities." Today the irreducible entities of any level are often called *holons* or *integrons*.[9]

Before the modern period it was believed that the universe was static and that, after a brief period of divine creation, it always had the same sort of hierarchical structure I have described. Supposedly, history began with Man, but in the nineteenth century it was realized that the entire universe has a history. In the twentieth century the discovery of the "Big Bang," as it is called, showed that the cosmic hierarchy I have described is the result of an enormous development. The universe began with just one class of elementary holons and then the higher ones developed one by one, terminating comparatively recently with the appearance of Man. Evolution is the history of the progressive development of the cosmic hierarchy.

The rational nature of Man depends on all the kinds of entities lower in the cosmic hierarchy. Sensate processes, which are very much like those exercised by other higher animals, support our rational thought. These sensate processes are in turn supported by the vital processes of neurons and other cells, which are in turn supported by the even more fundamental processes of inanimate matter. The sensate, vital, and inanimate entities involved in human processes have their own independence. Entities on the lower levels have been adapted to the higher ones, but they are essentially the same as the ones possessed by similar entities that are independent of Man. A pig's heart can take the place of a human heart, a mechanical contrivance a knee, Michael Polanyi has described the situation by comparing it with human speech;

It includes five levels; namely the production (1) of voice, (2) of words, (3) of sentences, (4) of style, and (5) of literary composition. Each of these levels is subject to its own laws, as prescribed (1) by phonetics, (2) by lexicography, (3) by grammar, (4) by stylistics, and (5) by literary criticism. These levels form a hierarchy of comprehensive entities, for the principles of each level operate under the control of the next higher level. The voice you produce is shaped into words by a vocabulary; a given vocabulary is shaped into sentences in accordance with grammar; and the sentences can he made to fit into a style, which in its turn is made to convey the ideas of a literary composition. Thus each level is subject to dual control; first, by the laws that apply to its elements in themselves and, second, by the laws that control the comprehensive entity formed by them.

Accordingly, the operation of a higher level cannot be accounted for by the laws governing its particulars forming the lower level. You cannot derive a vocabulary from phonetics; you cannot derive the grammar of a language from its vocabulary; a correct use of grammar does not account for good style; and the good style does not provide the content of a piece of prose. We may conclude then quite generally . . . that it is impossible to represent the organizing principles of a higher level by the laws governing its isolated particulars.[10]

Each independent level has its own laws, but at the same time it is adapted to the higher level above it. We can apply this to the present situation and speak of "sublation." Sublation is an original Hegelian term that is often used by modern theologians to mean that

what sublates goes beyond what is sublated, introduces something new and distinct, puts everything on a new basis, yet so far from interfering with the sublated or destroying it, on the contrary needs it, includes it, preserves all its proper features and properties, and carries them forward to a fuller realization within a richer context.[11]

I am applying the word to cosmology and claiming that in the cosmic hierarchy higher entities sublate lower ones. We know that the mystical body of Christ sublates human beings to be its members. Thereby they become something greater than they are of themselves. Similarly, in the Eucharist he sublates the matter of bread and wine so that, while retaining its "proper features and properties," they are carried "to a further realization within a richer context" of his cosmic body.

Thus, we are forced to qualify the statement of Schillebeeckx quoted above, that "a reality cannot at the same time be two realities" (E 74–75). One can say, depending on the context, that a reality is both a unique lower entity possessing its own laws, and at the same time a part of a higher one. In the mystical body, an independent human being can also be a member of the mystical Christ. In the Eucharist the complex of atoms and molecules that constitute bread can have its own mode of being even when it also becomes the Eucharistic body of Christ. At the moment of consecration, bread is sublated by Christ so that while retaining its own proper essence as bread it becomes part of his Eucharistic body. When it is sublated by the Lord it becomes capable of nourishing the soul of the communicant. Yet as bread it still continues to be a complex structure of inanimate atoms and molecules adapted to nourish the bodily life of human beings.

Thus the new knowledge of the modern era has forced us to speak in a different way than our ancestors did in previous ones. When we speak of the nature of the Eucharist, we say that the bread becomes part of Christ himself. If we are considering the ordinary philosophical nature of Eucharistic bread apart from its role in the Eucharist, we have to say that it remains "essentially" the same as before it was consecrated. But, of course, once consecrated, its highest property is its ability to contribute to the sanctifying activity of Christ himself. This ambiguity about the meaning of "essential" arises when one thinks about the role of a neuron in the human brain. Of itself, a neuron is "essentially" a one-celled organism. But at the same time it is contributing to human thought and desire in virtue of its higher essence. This case is pretty much, albeit on different levels, the same as in the case of the Eucharistic bread. The supernatural and miraculous aspect of the latter situation is that, by the power of the Spirit, the higher natural reality of the bread jumps several levels of the cosmic hierarchy to reach the highest one of all, the level of the incarnate Word.

The situation is quite similar to that of the "mystical body" of Christ. When a convert is baptized he becomes a part of Christ. Yet he does not change his ordinary philosophical essence. He is still, as far as his philosophical essence is concerned, a human being, but a human being who is united to Christ in a real way that can only be described by saying with St. Paul that he lives now, not he, but Christ lives in him (Gal. 2:20). Which is more important, his membership in the mystical body or his own philosophical essence? I think it is more important that he is part of Christ, and if one talks about his nature in the more important sense of the term, he no longer exists as himself but rather as part of Christ. This is something like what happens to the whole world in the case of Rahner's "supernatural existential." From the very beginning the "nature" of the world is a supernatural one in spite of the fact that it still has a philosophical essence that is merely natural in itself.

Is it wrong to say that transubstantiation changes the bread of the Mass into Christ himself, yet that at the same time the bread remains bread? I think not. There is no contradiction. No matter how miraculous the Eucharist is, there is no contradiction in holding that it has two "essences." The second, miraculous essence could be said, from one point of view, to be "accidental" rather than "essential." But that kind of language is inadequate. Our ordinary way of speaking does not suffice to express the nature of the Eucharist.

The reception of the Eucharist is a means by which human members of Christ are deified. Without losing their own nature they become his members. When in Heaven human beings become perfect, then they will be as pure and holy as the Eucharistic bread already is. The Parousia will be the time when the entire universe becomes completely subject to Christ. Right now ordinary matter is partially under the control of sinful human beings and demonic forces. When sin is ended and evil powers expelled from the world, then the universe itself will be fully the cosmic body of Christ, subject entirely to his wishes and to the freedom of the sons of God who are his members. The resurrected physical body of Christ is already subject to him. The state that we now desire for ourselves is the one in which the entire universe will be subject in the same way, including our own rational natures and the lower entities within us that are now partially independent of our wills.

The doctrine of the Eucharist was a stumbling block for the sixteenth century Church, The Council Fathers knew nothing about molecules or atoms, nor of the empirical evidence that supports their existence within human bodies. They simply used the best and clearest language they could find at the time. Schillebeeckx was correct when he said that they simply repeated the doctrine left to them from the Fathers of the Church in the best way available to them, which was in terms of Thomistic transubstantiation.

The philosophical theory suggested by St. Thomas was good for its time, and was even good at the time of Trent. But today, in the face of modern scientific evidence, it seems to be inadequate. The theory of the cosmic hierarchy I propose seems to be better. It shows that while he was on Earth the physical body of Christ contained within itself elementary particles, atoms, molecules, etc., just as ours does. Each of those subordinate entities has its own act of existing. Yet at the time of the consecration of the Mass they are sublated by the reality of Christ, who exists on the rational and cosmic levels.

In the *Catechism of the Catholic Church* (no. 1374) the Council of Trent is quoted as saying that *"the whole Christ is truly, really, and substantially* contained" in the Eucharist. Then it quotes the encyclical of Pope Paul VI, who tells us that Trent means to say that Jesus's presence is real in the fullest sense possible: "it is a substantial presence by which Christ, God and man, makes himself wholly and entirely present" *(Mysterium Fidei,* no. 39). That is the meaning of his words, "truly, really, and substantially." Pope Paul VI was not a physicist. He was simply repeating a doctrine that has come down from the Fathers of the Church, from a time in which molecules and atoms were unknown.

So what, then, is the meaning of the "species" of the bread and wine that Trent says remains after the consecration of the Mass? It has to be the reality of the bread and wine that has been sublated by the cosmic Christ as the real symbol by which he nourishes spiritually the members of the Church, his mystical body.

III. The Sacramental Universe

Having sketched a modern theory of transubstantiation we are now in a position to see more clearly its relationship to transignification. We can agree in a qualified sense with the statement of Schoonenberg that "transubstantiation takes place in a transignification, a transfinalization."[12] When they are consecrated, the Eucharistic species assume a new meaning and a new purpose in virtue of which they are able to function as the symbolic cause of the unity of the Church and the sanctification of the individual communicant. But the meaning they assume is a very special one. They now signify not only the unity of the Church but also the real local presence of Christ, his here-and-now availability as an object of worship and source of forgiveness, healing, and new life in the Spirit. They could not truly possess this meaning if the Lord were not really present, if the Eucharistic species did not already contain what they signify. Nor could the Church be one or the believer be sanctified in the powerful way the symbol intends if that were not the case. Transubstantiation, that is, the real presence of Christ himself in the Eucharistic species, is what makes transignification and transfinalization real.

As Pope Paul VI insisted in his 1965 encyclical, *Mysterium Fidei,* there is danger in using the term "transignification" if its connection with transubstantiation is not made apparent. The Eucharist is not only a symbolic reality, but also a cosmological reality, something which has to do with the temporal, spatial, and material world in which we live. Some modern philosophy is incapable of giving due weight to this cosmological aspect. For that we need a cosmology that synthesizes the subjective viewpoint not only with the more objective and empirical viewpoint of science, but also with the traditional doctrine of the Church.

"The language of transubstantiation . . . stresses the fact that the whole of creation is ultimately sacramental, that it has, in God's ordering of creation, a capacity to incarnate the action in which God gives His life to man" (Powers, 185–86). Because matter is by nature a potentially sacramental reality, the power of incarnating himself possessed by the Logos can reach out beyond his immediate personal body to transform the Eucharistic bread and wine, and through it the worshiping community. Ultimately this power will eventually transform the entire world. Thus, in his epistle to the Romans, St. Paul speaks of how the "creation itself will be set free from its bondage to decay and will obtain the freedom of the glory of the children of God. We know that the whole creation has been groaning in labor pains until now; and not only the creation but we ourselves, who have the first fruits of the Spirit, groan inwardly while we wait for adoption, the redemption of our bodies" (Rom. 8:21–23). The transformation of creation, which has already partially taken place in some persons, will ultimately envelop the world. As the cosmic body of the Logos himself it will receive the transforming power of his resurrection and become, if not part of the "mystical body" in the strict sense, at least so associated with it that it will share in "the glory of the children of God." The sign and promise of this final, eschatological transformation is the transformation of the Eucharistic bread and wine.

No one has expressed this more beautifully that Teilhard de Chardin in several of his short essays. In *The Mass on the World* he invited the Lord to empower him to pronounce over creation the transforming words, "This is my Body. . . . This is my Blood."[13] In another essay he describes the experience of an unnamed "friend," very likely himself, who kneeling before the Blessed Sacrament, "experienced a very strange impression" (op. cit., 47). As he watched and prayed, the host in the monstrance before him gradually began to expand its boundaries until it embraced the whole world, taking into itself, in the measure possible, the substance of all things.

Teilhard seems to have conveyed to us an insight that was entrusted to him for our scientific age. The universe, which scientists analyze and whose structure they have in some ways elucidated to an extent undreamed of by previous ages, is most profoundly understood in terms of the Eucharist. It is really the cosmic body of Christ, a reality destined to be glorified by being "eucharistized" or "transubstantiated." Therefore the history of the universe is a kind of Eucharist, a cosmic liturgy. The matter to be offered was prepared at creation and handed over to creatures as the priests of creation in order to be offered to the Father. Because of sin the offering was not made, until finally in the fullness of time the true high priest came and "entered once for all into the Holy Place, not with the blood of goats and calves, but with his own blood, thus obtaining eternal redemption" (Heb. 9:12). By and in the sacrifice of Jesus the whole material-spiritual universe has been offered and partially transformed. As yet the transforming power of this sacrifice has not completed its work, for we have not yet completed our own ratification of the offering. But we look for the coming of the day when our offering will be complete and he to whom it is offered will make all things new (Rev. 21:5). It will be made new in Jesus, for its deepest reality consists in the fact that it is his cosmic body which must ultimately share in his personal glorification.

At the present time, the ecological crisis demands from us special emphasis on the cosmic aspect of the Eucharistic symbolism. Knowing that Earth and universe find their unity and deepest reality in Christ, we must learn to respect their integrity and strive to become the stewards and priests rather than the exploiters of creation. By eating the Eucharistic bread we strengthen our sense of dependence upon the world and our unity with it. It is a sacramental symbol of Christ's sharing of his life with us, which is worthy of our profound reverence.

This realization enables us to put our modern scientific knowledge of the world into perspective. Science is a wonderful gift of God but it will not fulfill the purpose for which God gave it to us until it is taken up into the higher wisdom given only by our offering of "the Mass on the world." As our emerging planetary civilization learns to offer this Mass, the reductionistic hardness, which is due to exclusive attention to the mechanisms of the world, will be ameliorated and we will become open to a more humane attitude.

This will reflect upon our understanding of the meaning or purpose of science's twin, technology, and of the other modern techniques that extend the spirit of technology into the social and economic life of our race. The construction and use of mechanisms will be seen as ordered to the integrated wholeness of human existence and of all creation in the Logos, as a precious service rendered to goals and strivings which far exceed the realm of the merely technological. The myth of the machine, the glorification of mechanisms for their own sake, will give way to an ideal of service and worship, the cosmic *opus Dei,* in which material, social, and economic techniques support and facilitate spiritual aspirations and divine glory.

NOTES

1. J. Neuner and J. Dupuis, eds., *The Christian Faith,* rev. ed. (New York: Alba House, 1982), no. 1527.

2. Edward Schillebeeckx, *The Eucharist* [= E] (London: Sheed & Ward, 1968), 54.

3. Piet Schoonenberg, "Transubstantiation" [= T], *Concilium* 24 (1967): 78–91, here 83.

4. William B. Ashworth Jr., "Catholicism and Early Modern Science," in *God and Nature,* ed. David C. Lindberg and Ronald L. Numbers (Berkeley: University of California Press, 1986), chap. 5, p. 151. Also Frederick Copleston, *A History of Philosophy,* 9 vols. (New York: Doubleday, 1985), 4:126–28.

5. Joseph M. Powers, *Eucharistic Theology* (New York: Herder & Herder, 1967), 166.

6. Robert J. Russell, William R. Stoeger, and George V. Coyne, eds., *Physics, Philosophy, and Theology* (Vatican City: Vatican Observatory, 1988 [distributed except in Italy and Vatican City by University of Notre Dame Press]), M1–M14.

7. Col. 1:15–20; Eph. 1:9–10, 20–23; and Rom. 8:19–23. Along with these, John 1:1–5 and Heb. 1:3–4, as well as 1 Cor. 8:6 and Phil. 2:6–11, have similar cosmic import.

8. *The Anchor Bible Dictionary,* ed. David Noel Freedman, 6 vols. (New York: Doubleday, 1992), 1:771.

9. Ernst Mayr, *This Is Biology: The Science of the Living World* (Cambridge, MA: Belknap Press of Harvard University Press, 1997), 19, citing François Jacob, *The Logic of Life: A History of Heredity* (New York: Pantheon, 1973), 302.

10. Michael Polanyi, *The Tacit Dimension* (Garden City, NY: Doubleday-Anchor, 1967), 35–36. Of course, Polanyi's analogy does not prove but rather illustrates his point of view.

11. Bernard Lonergan, *Method in Theology* (New York: Herder & Herder, 1972), 241.

12. Powers, *Eucharistic Theology,* 173.

13. Pierre Teilhard de Chardin, *Hymn of the Universe,* trans. Gerald Vann (New York: Harper Torchbooks, 1965), 19–37, esp. 23.

DIE MESSE ÜBER DIE WELT

I.   Eucharistie-Theologie und Kosmologie

II.   Transsubstantiation

III.   Das sakramentale Universum

      Anmerkungen

Die Messe über die Welt

D er vorliegende Beitrag umfasst drei Abschnitte. Der erste erörtert das Verhältnis der theologischen Theorie der Transsubstantiation zu der der *Transsignifikation* (Änderung der Bedeutung) und der *Transfinalisation* (Änderung der Finalität). Die letzten beiden Theorien wurden von nordeuropäischen Theologen unmittelbar vor dem Zweiten Vatikanischen Konzil ausformuliert. Im zweiten Abschnitt wird eine ganzheitliche Sicht des Wesens der Materie dargelegt. Unsere heutigen wissenschaftlichen Kenntnisse scheinen es unumgänglich zu machen, sich von der aristotelischen Theorie des Hylemorphismus zugunsten einer Theorie zu verabschieden, derzufolge reale Wesen einer bestimmten Ebene reale, aber untergeordnete Wesen niedrigerer Ebene „aufheben". So ist zum Beispiel ein Mensch eine Substanz, die in sich selbst viele kleinere Substanzen enthält. Der physische Leib Christi enthielt in sich, als er fleischliche Gestalt angenommen hatte, eine große Zahl wechselseitig miteinander verbundener Atome und Moleküle. Der dritte Abschnitt erörtert Gedanken Pierre Teilhard de Chardin's zum Verhältnis von Christus zur Materie.

I. EUCHARISTIE-THEOLOGIE UND KOSMOLOGIE

Im 16. Jahrhundert hat das Konzil von Trient die Lehre der Kirche zur Eucharistie in einer Weise festgeschrieben, die den Standpunkt der aristotelisch-thomasischen Begrifflichkeit vorauszusetzen schien:

Wer sagt, im hochheiligen Sakrament der Eucharistie verbliebe zusammen mit dem Leib und Blut unseres Herrn Jesus Christus die Substanz des Brotes und des Weines, und jene wunderbare und einzigartige Verwandlung der ganzen Substanz des Brotes in den Leib und der ganzen Substanz des Weines in das Blut, wobei lediglich die Gestalten von Brot und Wein bleiben, leugnet – und zwar nennt die katholische Kirche diese Wandlung sehr treffend Wesensverwandlung –: der sei mit dem Anathema belegt.[1]

Die leichteste und klarste Weise, diese Lehre zu verstehen, bot die scholastische Auffassung von Substanz und Akzidens. Aristoteles zufolge existieren Akzidenzien in und durch Substanzen; sie qualifizieren diese in unterschiedlicher Weise. Der heilige Thomas meinte, dass die Eucharistie den einzigartigen Fall darstelle, bei der eine Substanz in eine andere verwandelt würde, ohne dass die Akzidenzien der ursprünglichen Substanz verschwinden. Durch die wundertätige Macht Gottes bleiben die Akzidenzien von Brot und Wein auch noch bestehen, nachdem die Substanz, der sie angehörten, verschwunden war. Wie dies sein konnte, war natürlich sehr schwer einzusehen, doch damals erwartete niemand, die Eucharistie vollkommen zu begreifen.

Doch das Konzilsdekret von Trient benutzte in Wahrheit nicht den aristotelischen Ausdruck „Akzidens", sondern stattdessen das lateinische „species", einen weniger klaren Terminus, der eine objektive Bedeutung im Sinne von „Akzidens" oder eine eher subjektive Bedeutung im Sinne von „Erscheinung" haben konnte. Ob die *species* objektiv wie die aristotelischen Akzidenzien oder eher wie subjektive Erscheinungen aufzufassen sind, ist nicht unmittelbar klar.

Können wir das als einen Hinweis darauf verstehen, dass das Konzil von Trient Vorsicht walten ließ und den Aristotelismus oder irgendeine andere philosophische Theorie nicht unterstützen wollte und dass deshalb folgerichtig nicht nur „species", sondern auch „Substanz" in einem sehr weiten, allgemeinen Sinn gedeutet werden wollte? Bald nach dem Zweiten Vatikanischen Konzil behauptete Edward Schillebeeckx, dass genau dies der Meinung der meisten Historiker vom Trienter Konzil entspreche.[2] Doch seine eigene Auffassung war komplexer. Während es seiner Meinung nach zwar stimmt, dass das Tridentinum den Aristotelismus nicht zur offiziellen Doktrin erheben wollte, war das Denken der Konzilsväter zwangsläufig an den aristotelischen begrifflichen Bezugsrahmen gebunden, den sich die meisten von ihnen im Zuge ihrer Ausbildung angeeignet hatten. Nur unter Benutzung der Kategorien des Aristotelismus waren sie in der Lage, ihren Glauben an die Realpräsenz Christi in der Eucharistie zum Ausdruck zu bringen.

In einem Artikel aus dem Jahr 1967 sagte Schillebeeckx' niederländischer Kollege Piet Schoonenberg mehr oder weniger dasselbe: „Daraus sieht man, dass die Glaubensformulierung eines Konzils, wie die jedermanns, niemals adäquat von einer zeitgebundenen theologischen Interpretation zu trennen ist. Sicherlich nicht für jene selbst, die sie aussprechen. Für uns aber, die später kommen, ist dies, wenigstens teilweise, möglich."[3]

Die Unterscheidung zwischen einer grundlegenden dogmatischen Wahrheit und deren Formulierung macht die Dogmengeschichte in Bezug auf die Eucharistie bereits vor dem Tridentinum deutlich. Schillebeeckx zufolge können innerhalb der Lehre des Thomas von Aquin zur Eucharistie aus dem 13. Jahrhundert drei Ebenen unterschieden werden: 1) die Ebene des *Glaubens* an die Realpräsenz; 2) die Ebene, auf der eine wirklich *ontologische* Veränderung der eucharistischen *species* behauptet wird; 3) die Ebene, auf der diese ontologische Veränderung mithilfe aristotelischer Kategorien zum Ausdruck gebracht wird [EG 41]. Schillebeeckx behauptete, dass die aristotelischen Kategorien heute als unangemessen betrachtet werden können, und deshalb müsse man die Lehre des Thomas von Aquin beiseite legen. Doch wie verhält es sich mit der ontologischen Ebene? Der Glaube an eine ontologische Veränderung des eucharistischen Brotes und Weines geht auf die griechischen Kirchenväter zurück. Schillebeeckx sagte, diese dachten dabei nicht an Substanz im aristotelischen Sinne, sondern im Sinne eines unabhängigen Seienden oder einer fundamentalen Wirklichkeit. Die Art und Weise, wie der Logos von den eucharistischen Elementen Besitz ergreift, war für sie vergleichbar mit seiner Besitzergreifung des Schoßes seiner Mutter, der Jungfrau Maria. Beide Ereignisse wurden von der Kraft des Heiligen

Geistes bewirkt. Für die Kirchenväter verloren deshalb Brot und Wein
in der Eucharistie ihre unabhängige Wirklichkeit oder Substanz und
wurden zum Leib und zum Blut Christi. Der Glaube der griechischen
Kirchenväter war im grundlegenden Sinne derselbe wie der der Trienter
Konzilsväter, er wurde jedoch in anderen, nicht aristotelischen Kategorien zum Ausdruck gebracht. Es geht um eine wirkliche ontologische
Veränderung der eucharistischen Elemente, und diese Veränderung ist es,
die der Eucharistie ihren besonderen Charakter verleiht. Es gibt demnach
eine grundlegende nicht-aristotelische Bedeutung von „Substanz" innerhalb der Tradition, die schließlich im Tridentinum mündete.

> Dass es nach der Konsekration keine *Wirklichkeit* Brot gibt, war wesent-
> lich und fundamental für das Glaubensdogma. Denn wenn die endgül-
> tige in der Eucharistie vorhandene *Wirklichkeit* Brot genannt wird,
> dann ist schlechthin Brot da (eine Wirklichkeit ist nicht zugleich zwei
> Wirklichkeiten!), und dann kann die eucharistische Gegenwart nur
> symbolisch aufgefasst werden. […] Nur zur Erklärung des „Bleibens
> der Gestalt kommt in den Gedanken der Konzilsväter die Lehre von der
> Substanz und den Akzidenzien auf, sodass sie, wenn sie im traditionel-
> len Sinne von der Brot-„Substanz" sprechen, in ihren Gedanken unver-
> meidlich den Gegensatz zu Akzidenzien herstellen. [EG 48–49]

Selbst wenn man also auf die aristotelische Formulierung verzichten
kann, so behauptet das Verständnis des Tridentinums von der eucharistischen Gegenwart nicht nur deren Wirklichkeit, es fordert auch eine
ontologische Veränderung der eucharistischen Elemente, „… d. h.: das
Vorhandensein eines ontologischen Moments in der sakramentalen
Darreichung des von Christus gesegneten Brotes ist zweifellos eine
Glaubensgegebenheit und nicht ein Einkleidungsaspekt" [EG 54]. Schillebeeckx zog also die Schlussfolgerung, dass das Konzil von Trient nicht
in aristotelisch-thomasischen Kategorien neu gedeutet werden muss.
Dennoch dachte er sehr wohl, dass es eine ontologische Veränderung in
Bezug auf die eucharistischen Elemente geben muss, so wie es auch im
Denken der Kirchenväter eine ontologische Veränderung in Bezug auf
die Herausbildung des Leibes Christi im Schoß der Jungfrau Maria gegeben haben musste.

Das Verhältnis von Eucharistie und kosmologischen Theorien blieb für die katholische Orthodoxie noch lange nach dem Trienter Konzil ein Problem. Die vorherrschende Schule gegenreformatorischen Denkens deutete das grundlegende Dogma mithilfe der relativ klaren (wenn auch gleichzeitig rätselhaften) aristotelisch-thomasischen Theorie des Hylemorphismus und war in einem Zeitalter heftigen Streits um die Religion nicht geneigt, alternative Auffassungen hierzu zu tolerieren. So wurden etwa im Jahr 1663 René Descartes' *Meditations* auf den römischen Index der verbotenen Bücher gesetzt, weil seine Auffassung von Materie als unvereinbar mit der Lehre von der Eucharistie betrachtet wurde.[4] Unser Jahrhundert ist natürlich sowohl, was theologische, als auch, was naturwissenschaftliche Theorien betrifft, weniger naiv als das siebzehnte. Wir fordern auch nicht so viel Übereinstimmung zwischen Physik und Theologie wie frühere Epochen. Dennoch ist dasselbe Grundproblem in unserer Zeit wieder aufgetaucht. Schillebeeckx schreibt:

> Schon zwischen den beiden Weltkriegen wurde es klar, dass die Transsubstantiation einer neuen Interpretation bedurfte. Die Ergebnisse der modernen Physik erschütterten die neuscholastischen Spekulationen in ihren Grundfesten. [...] Zwischen den beiden Weltkriegen erschien eine fast unübersehbare Flut von Literatur über die Konsequenzen der positiven Wissenschaften für das traditionelle Verständnis der Eucharistie. [...] Weil die Theologen, welche die Errungenschaften dieser neuen Wissenschaft in den Substanzbegriff eingliedern wollten, zu aussichtslosen Schlussfolgerungen kamen und ihr Ausgangspunkt gerade der war, dass eine ontologische Verwandlung die physische Realität nicht unverletzt lassen konnte, haben sie selbst am meisten zu der Einsicht beigetragen, dass eine naturontologische Interpretation der Eucharistie unhaltbar sei. [EG 62–63]

Diese wachsende Überzeugung war einer der Faktoren, die zur Aneignung eines anderen, eher personalistischen Ansatzes vonseiten nordeuropäischer Theologen nach dem Zweiten Weltkrieg führten. Ein weiterer Faktor waren zeitgenössische Entwicklungen innerhalb der Philosophie, die neue Kategorien erforderlich machten, welche besser dafür geeignet zu sein schienen, das menschliche und symbolische

Wesen der Sakramente allgemein und der Eucharistie im Besonderen
zum Ausdruck zu bringen. Existenzialistisches, phänomenologisches
und hermeneutisches Denken funktioniert nicht in der ontischen
Weise, wie sie den Naturwissenschaften eignet, sondern vollzieht sich
innerhalb eines hauptsächlich von subjektiver menschlicher Erfahrung,
personaler und symbolischer Entfaltung seiner selbst und interperso-
naler Kommunikation bestimmten Horizonts. Innerhalb dieses Horizonts wird das Handeln Christi in der Eucharistie eher im Sinne von
Bedeutung und symbolischem Selbstausdruck als im Sinne der eher
objektiven und kosmologischen Begriffe der Neuscholastik gesehen.
Die Veränderung, die sich mit den eucharistischen Elementen von Brot
und Wein bei der Wandlung in der Messe vollzieht, wird folglich eher
als Veränderung der Bedeutung und des Zwecks, und nicht der Substanz verstanden. So werden nun die Ausdrücke „Transignifikation"
(Änderung der Bedeutung) und „Transfinalisation" (Änderung der
Finalität) eher benutzt als der der traditionellen „Transsubstantiation"
(Änderung der Substanz).

Doch dieser anthropologische Ansatz ist mit Schwierigkeiten verbunden. Im Jahr 1965 promulgierte Papst Paul VI. seine Enzyklika *Mysterium fidei*. Unter den Meinungen, zu denen er darin Stellung bezog,
war auch die Behauptung, dass die Änderung der Bedeutung oder Finalität (Zielbestimmung) der eucharistischen Elemente, die aus deren Rolle
innerhalb der symbolischen und sakramentalen Handlung der Messe
resultiert, eine angemessene Erklärung der Transsubstantiation darstelle.
Seiner Ansicht nach zeigt die verbindliche Lehrtradition der Kirche, dass
mit den konsekrierten *species* eine ontologische Veränderung vonstatten
gehe, die das übersteigt, was mit „Bedeutung" und „Symbol" zur Sprache
gebracht werden kann. Der traditionelle Terminus „Transsubstantiation"
bringt dies zum Ausdruck und kann nicht zugunsten von Transsignifikation oder Transfinalisation aufgegeben werden.

Schillebeeckx und Schoonenberg antworteten auf solche kritischen
Bemerkungen zur Transsignifikation in unterschiedlicher Weise. In
einem Kommentar zu *Mysterium fidei* unterscheidet Schoonenberg zwischen zwei Arten von Zeichenhandlungen:

Es gibt Zeichenhandlungen, die etwas *zur Kenntnis bringen*, was der Belehrung, dem Erwecken von Gefühlen oder der Übermittlung einer Instruktion oder eines Befehls dient (man denke an die Verkehrssignale). Es gibt aber auch Zeichen – und hier ist vor allem die Zeichen-*handlung* das Primäre –, bei welchen das zur Kenntnis Gebrachte zugleich mitgeteilt oder wenigstens angeboten wird. Der Inhalt dieser zweiten Art von Zeichen ist immer eine Form der Liebe oder der Gemeinschaft: Man denke hier an Händedruck, Kuss, usw. Diese zweite Art kann voll und ganz mit dem Namen „wirkendes Zeichen" genannt werden, obwohl auch die erste Art wirksam ist, zunächst durch Mitteilung einer Erkenntnis, und auch, indem man auch in ihnen untereinander in Gemeinschaft tritt, wenngleich in sehr indirekter Weise. Wir können so einerseits von *informierenden* und andererseits von *gemeinschaftsbildenden* [kommunizierend] Zeichen sprechen. [T 310]

Schoonenberg zufolge hatte *Mysterium fidei* lediglich informative Zeichen im Sinn, wenn die Enzyklika in Abrede stellte, dass die Transsubstantiation der eucharistischen *species* mit „Transsignifikation" erfasst werden könne. Doch die Eucharistie ist ein gemeinschaftsbildendes Zeichen, „unter welchem der Herr seinen Leib gibt, um uns zu seinem Leib zu machen, worin er sich selbst zur Gemeinschaft mit ihm und in ihm uns schenkt" [T 310].

Schillebeeckx reagierte in anderer Weise. Er stimmte mit Schoonenberg und dem englischen Theologen Charles Davis darin überein, wie wichtig und nützlich der anthropologische Ansatz für das Verständnis der Eucharistie sei, doch er stellte die Frage: „Fällt die Transsignifikation mit der Transsubstantiation zusammen, oder ist sie deren Folge oder Implikation? Was sich hier in aller Tragweite auftut, ist letztlich die Frage nach der Wirklichkeit" [EG 97]. Seine Antwort darauf lautet: „Mit Recht sehen einige Autoren die Schöpfung, den Beginn des Gnadenbundes, als den Hintergrund auch des eucharistischen Geschehens" [EG 84]. Vor dem Hintergrund der Tradition der Kirche und im Lichte dieses Grundsatzes konnte er anmerken:

. . . in gläubiger Ehrfurcht vor dem, was das katholische Glaubens*bekenntnis* seit Jahrhunderten in der eucharistischen Feier erfahren lässt, kann ich mich persönlich nicht mit einer *bloß* phänomenologischen Interpretation ohne metaphysische Dichte zufriedengeben. Die Wirklichkeit ist kein Gemächte des Menschen: In diesem Sinne ist Realismus wesentlich für den christlichen Glauben. Bei meiner Neuinterpretation der Gegebenheit des Tridentinismus komme ich deshalb auch nie klar mit einer Berufung auf allein menschliche *Sinn-Stiftung*, auch nicht, wenn man diese in den Glauben verlegt. Eine solche Transsignifikation hat natürlich einen Platz in der Eucharistie, aber sie wird getragen und hervorgerufen durch die neuschaffende Tätigkeit des Heiligen Geistes, des Geistes Christi, vom Vater gesandt. Im Raum der aktiv glaubenden, handelnden und feiernden Kirche *handelt* Gott selbst; das Ereignis dieses Heilshandelns Gottes ist sakramental eine „neue Schöpfung", die unsere eschatologische Beziehung zum Reich Gottes beständig macht und vertieft. [EG 102]

Mit seinem Satz „Die Wirklichkeit ist kein Gemächte des Menschen" deckt Schillebeeckx die entscheidende Schwäche des Versuchs auf, die Eucharistie vollständig im Sinne der Transsignifikation zu erklären. Wenn ein junger Mann seiner Verlobten einen Ring schenkt, dann verändert sein symbolisches Handeln die menschliche Situation in sehr bedeutender Weise.[5] Doch es hat keine Auswirkungen auf die physische Beschaffenheit des Rings. Man mag vielleicht sagen, dass dies die „relationale Wirklichkeit" des Rings verändert, doch eine solche Veränderung genügt nicht, um den Sinngehalt der kirchlichen Lehrtradition zur Eucharistie zum Ausdruck zu bringen. Der verherrlichte Christus kann sich selbst in einer Vollkommenheit und Macht hingeben, wie es gewöhnlichen Menschen nicht möglich ist, und – so Schillebeeckx – seine eucharistische Selbsthingabe ist eine Gabe seiner selbst und nicht „Selbsthingabe *im* Geschenk" [EG 93]. Die Analogie zwischen dem menschlichen Geben eines Geschenks und Christi Geschenk der Selbsthingabe in der Eucharistie ist zu weit hergeholt und zu schwach, um eine angemessene erklärende Kraft zu haben.

Schoonenberg weicht der Notwendigkeit aus, eine Kosmologie zu entwerfen, die unsere modernen naturwissenschaftlichen Kenntnisse ernst nimmt und auch Kategorien für das Verständnis der Transsubstantiation liefert. Die Behauptung, dass ein materieller Gegenstand einzig und allein deshalb eine Wesensverwandlung durchmacht, indem er eine bestimmte Rolle innerhalb einer Zeichenhandlung einnimmt, ist zu schwach. Die Unzufriedenheit damit, wie sie in *Mysterium fidei* zum Ausdruck kommt, besteht nicht ohne Grund. Auch wenn die aristotelisch-scholastische Kosmologie unangemessen ist, so bringt die Lehre von der Transsubstantiation weiterhin die Sorge der Kirche um die Realität der Materie und den echten Anteil am Dasein zum Ausdruck, den die Materie auch auf spiritueller Ebene hat. Wenn Materie in Ideen hinein aufgelöst wird, dann wird sie spirituelle Wirklichkeit selbst in ein Wunschdenken und fromme Sehnsüchte hinein verdampfen.

Schillebeeckx' Schlussfolgerung, dass Transsignifikation der Transsubstantiation nicht gleichwertig oder mit ihr identisch ist, ist ohne Zweifel richtig. Doch er geht nicht sehr weit darin, das „wie" der eucharistischen Gegenwart zu erklären, wenn er auch darauf beharrt, dass es tatsächlich untrennbar von ihr ist [EG 103–4]. Im Mittelalter war das Problem des Verhältnisses zwischen Eucharistietheologie und Kosmologie unausweichlich gegeben, aber auch unlösbar im Lichte der allgemeinen Annahme, dass die Theorie des Hylemorphismus zutreffend ist. Nun aber ist uns eine andere Theorie der Materie erschlossen. In unserer Zeit kommt die Theologie nicht umhin, die Naturwissenschaft mit in Betracht zu ziehen, und wir müssen – darauf beharrte Papst Johannes Paul II. – lernen, damit umzugehen.[6] Wenn es nicht gelingt, kosmologische Überlegungen in die Theologie mit aufzunehmen, dann wird Letztere ätherisch oder idealistisch. Wir können nicht einfach vergessen, was wir über die Struktur der Materie wissen.

Mir scheint, dass heute der Stand der Fragestellung zur Transsubstantiation im Wesentlichen derselbe ist wie ihn uns Papst Paul VI., Schillebeeckx und Schoonenberg in den 1960er-Jahren hinterlassen haben. Die Theologen haben ihre Aufmerksamkeit verschiedenen anderen Aspekten der Eucharistie zugewandt, doch die verwirrende aufgeworfene Frage bleibt nach wie vor bestehen. Ich vermute, dass ein Grund hierfür der ist, dass es die meisten Theologen vermeiden, über naturwissenschaftliche Fragen nachzudenken, und dass umgekehrt die meisten Naturwissenschaftler theologischen Fragen ausweichen. Doch ich will mich nun jedenfalls der Aufgabe widmen, eine befriedigende moderne Deutung der Transsubstantiation vorzulegen.

II. Transsubstantiation

Das Neue Testament benutzt den Ausdruck „Leib" in Bezug auf Christus in mindestens dreifach unterschiedlicher Weise: Jesus ist ein Mensch und hat deshalb einen physischen Leib. Er ist zuinnerst verbunden und identisch mit der Kirche, und deshalb hat er auch einen mystischen Leib. In der Eucharistiefeier essen wir seinen Leib; er hat also auch einen eucharistischen Leib. Dazu kommt möglicherweise noch ein vierter Leib, auf den im Neuen Testament Bezug genommen wird. Teilhard de Chardin wurde von verschiedenen berühmten Textstellen bei Paulus inspiriert, die von der kosmischen Dimension und Rolle Christi sprechen.[7] Eine davon ist Kol 1,15–20, möglicherweise eine adaptierte Fassung eines frühchristlichen Hymnus, der das Herrsein Christi über die ganze Schöpfung pries. Dieser Hymnus scheint behauptet zu haben, dass er das Haupt des Leibes ist, was in diesem Zusammenhang den kosmischen Leib meint, dem im hellenistischen Denken eine herausragende Rolle zukommt.[8] Im kanonischen Text des Kolosserbriefes hat der Autor die Veränderung vorgenommen, dass sich „Leib" auf die Kirche bezieht. Doch dies hat anscheinend dem allgemeinen Verständnis im Kolosserbrief vom Verhältnis zwischen Christus und dem Kosmos keinen Abbruch getan, das ich selbst hier in der Weise zum Ausdruck bringe, dass ich sage, er hat einen „kosmischen Leib", um ihn von seinem „mystischen Leib", der Kirche, zu unterscheiden.

Diese vier Leiber Christi sind natürlich eng miteinander verbunden. Ich bringe das dadurch zum Ausdruck, dass ich sage, sie sind „inadäquat unterschieden". Ihre Unterscheidung verhindert die Tatsache nicht, dass sie eine einzige Wirklichkeit bilden, denn die vier Leiber sind Aspekte der umfassenden Wirklichkeit des inkarnierten Logos. Wie wir noch sehen werden, bildet jeder Leib ein gemeinsames Muster aus, das in jedem Fall etwas unterschiedlich ausfällt.

Um dies zu verstehen, muss man meiner Meinung nach zunächst das begreifen, was ich „die kosmische Hierarchie" nenne. Die moderne Naturwissenschaft hat entdeckt, dass es im Menschen eine Hierarchie kleinerer Einheiten, nämlich Organismen, Organe und Gewebe, Zellen, Moleküle, Atome, Nukleone (d. h. Protonen und Neutronen), Elektronen und Quarks gibt, und nun forscht man sogar nach noch kleineren. Alle Einheiten innerhalb dieser Hierarchie setzen sich auf jeder Ebene außer der untersten aus einer oder mehreren Entitäten aus einer darunter liegenden Ebene zusammen.

Eine entscheidende Frage ist es, ob eine bestimmte Entität auf die in ihr enthaltenen Entitäten „reduziert" werden kann oder nicht. Welche Arten von Entitäten können restlos auf solche auf einer niedrigeren Ebene reduziert werden, und welche nicht? Wenn man sagt, dass eine bestimmte Entität irreduzibel ist, dann meint man damit, dass sie einzigartige Eigenschaften einer „höheren Ebene" aufweist, die nicht aus den in ihr enthaltenen untergeordneten Entitäten erklärt werden können. Diese niedrigeren Entitäten leisten ihren Beitrag zu den Eigenschaften der höheren Ebene, doch Letztere hat etwas, was darüber hinausgeht. In ihrer Wirkweise entfaltet sie eine höhere Qualität – und auf den höheren Ebenen ein einheitsstiftendes Bewusstsein –, die niemals mithilfe der in ihr enthaltenen untergeordneten Größen erklärt werden kann. Andererseits gilt: Wenn eine Entität reduzierbar ist, dann kann sie vollständig durch die niedrigeren Entitäten erklärt werden. In diesem Fall ist das scheinbar einheitliche Wirken der höheren Entität vollständig auf die Interaktion der kleineren Einheiten zurückzuführen.

In unserem theologischen Kontext können wir davon ausgehen, dass vernunftbegabte Wesen wie wir selbst nicht auf niedrigere Ebenen reduziert werden können. Ich gehe in der Tat davon aus, dass die meisten Leserinnen und Leser meiner Behauptung zustimmen, dass es eine Reihe irreduzibler Ebenen innerhalb der natürlichen Hierarchie gibt. Ich meine, dass dazu wenigstens die Ebenen des Unbelebten, des Belebten, des Empfindsamen und des Rationalen sowie auch die kosmische Ebene gehört, deren einzigartige Entität der kosmische Christus ist. Meiner Meinung nach gibt es auch eine niedrigste und bis jetzt unbekannte elementare unbelebte Ebene. Es ist gut möglich, dass es noch mehr Ebenen gibt, aber für unsere Zwecke genügt es, die sechs eben erwähnten in Betracht zu ziehen. Die Entität einer bestimmten Ebene hat eine wesenhafte Eigenart, über die keine der niedrigeren Ebene verfügt. So können weder ein vernunftbegabtes Wesen wie der Mensch noch ein empfindsames Wesen wie etwa ein Hund vollständig mithilfe der Bestandteile, aus denen sie sich zusammensetzen, erklärt werden. Die kleinsten Entitäten der niedrigsten, unbelebten Ebene sind natürlich irreduzibel. Es sind die „Atome" der alten Griechen, aus denen alles besteht. Ich nenne sie „elementare Entitäten". Heute werden die irreduziblen Entitäten jeder Ebene oft *Holons* oder *Integrons* genannt.[9]

Vor der Moderne glaubte man, dass das Universum statisch sei und dass es nach einer kurzen Zeitspanne der Erschaffung durch Gott immer dieselbe Art von hierarchischer Struktur aufgewiesen habe, die ich beschrieben habe. Die Geschichte begann – so nahm man an – mit dem Menschen. Doch im 19. Jahrhundert erkannte man, dass das gesamte Universum eine Geschichte hat. Im 20. Jahrhundert zeigte die Entdeckung des sogenannten Urknalls, dass die von mir beschriebene kosmische Hierarchie das Ergebnis einer unvorstellbar umfassenden Entwicklungsgeschichte ist. Das Universum begann mit lediglich einer Klasse elementarer Holons, und dann gingen die höheren nach und nach daraus hervor. Diese Entwicklung erreichte vergleichsweise erst vor Kurzem ihren Endpunkt mit dem Menschen. Die Evolution ist die Geschichte der fortschreitenden Entwicklung der kosmischen Hierarchie.

Die Vernunftnatur des Menschen hängt von allen Arten innerhalb der kosmischen Hierarchie niedriger angesiedelter Entitäten ab. Sensitive Prozesse, die denen von höheren Lebewesen sehr ähnlich sind, unterstützen unser rationales Denken. Diese sensitiven Prozesse werden wiederum von vitalen Prozessen der Neuronen und anderer Zellen unterstützt, die ihrerseits wiederum auf grundlegenden Vorgängen auf der Ebene unbelebter Materie beruhen. Die sensitiven, vitalen und unbelebten Entitäten, die an menschlichen Prozessen beteiligt sind, haben ihre eigene Unabhängigkeit. Entitäten auf niedrigerer Ebene wurden an die höheren angeglichen, doch sie sind im Wesentlichen dieselben, wie sie ähnliche Entitäten aufweisen, die unabhängig vom Menschen sind. Das

Herz eines Schweines kann das eines Menschen ersetzen, ein mechanischer Apparat kann an die Stelle des Kniegelenks treten. Michael Polanyi hat diese Situation mittels eines Vergleichs mit der menschlichen Sprache, mit dem Halten einer Rede, erläutert:

> Fünf Ebenen sind dabei im Spiel, nämlich die Erzeugung 1) der Stimme, 2) der Wörter, 3) der Sätze, 4) des Stils und 5) der literarischen Komposition. Jede dieser Ebenen ist ihren eigenen Gesetzen unterworfen, wie sie 1) von der Phonetik, 2) der Lexik, 3) der Grammatik, 4) der Stilistik und 5) von der Literaturkritik vorgegeben werden. Diese Ebenen bilden eine Hierarchie komplexer Entitäten, denn die Prinzipien, die auf eine Ebene jeweils anwendbar sind, stehen unter der Aufsicht der nächsthöheren. Die erzeugten Laute werden vermittels eines Vokabulars zu Wörtern geformt; aus einem gegebenen Vokabular werden im Einklang mit einer Grammatik Sätze gebildet; die Sätze müssen zu einem Stil passen, in dem wiederum die Ideen einer literarischen Komposition zum Ausdruck kommen sollen. Folglich unterliegt jede Ebene einer doppelten Kontrolle: erstens derjenigen durch die Gesetze, die für die Elemente selbst gelten, und zweitens der Kontrolle durch die Gesetze, denen die aus diesen Elementen gebildete komplexe Entität untersteht.
>
> Dementsprechend können die Gesetze der Elemente einer unteren Ebene nicht von den Operationen einer höheren Ebene Rechenschaft geben. Aus der Phonetik lässt sich noch kein Vokabular ableiten, aus dem Vokabular einer Sprache nicht eine Grammatik; ein korrekter Gebrauch der Grammatik bietet noch keine Gewähr für guten Stil, und ein solcher sorgt noch nicht für den gedanklichen Gehalt eines Prosastücks. Wir können daraus den allgemeinen Schluss ziehen [. . .], dass sich die Organisationsprinzipien einer höheren Ebene nicht mit den Mitteln der für ihre einzelnen Bestandteile gültigen Gesetze darstellen lassen.[10]

Jede unabhängige Ebene hat ihre je eigenen Gesetze, doch zugleich wird sie der höheren Ebene angeglichen. Wir können dies auf die gegenwärtige Situation anwenden und von „Aufhebung" sprechen. Aufhebung ist ein Ausdruck, der ursprünglich auf Hegel zurückgeht und oftmals von modernen Theologen in dem Sinne benutzt wird, dass

…jede folgende Ebene die vorhergehenden Ebenen aufhebt, indem sie über sie hinausgeht, ein höheres Prinzip aufstellt, neue Vollzüge einführt, die Integrität der vorhergehenden Ebenen wahrt und zugleich ihre Reichweite und Bedeutung enorm erweitert.[11]

Ich wende diesen Ausdruck auf die Kosmologie an und behaupte, dass innerhalb der kosmischen Hierarchie höhere Entitäten niedrigere aufheben. Wir wissen, dass der mystische Leib Christi die Menschen aufhebt, damit sie seine Glieder sind. Damit werden sie etwas Größeres, als sie von sich aus sind. In ähnlicher Weise hebt er bei der Eucharistie die Materie von Brot und Wein auf, sodass sie zwar ihre eigentümlichen Charakteristika und Eigenschaften (d. h. „die Integrität der vorhergehenden Ebenen") beibehalten, aber auf die Stufe einer weiteren Verwirklichung innerhalb eines reichhaltigeren Kontextes seines kosmischen Leibes gehoben werden, oder in ihrer „Reichweite und Bedeutung enorm erweitert" werden.

Wir sind deshalb gezwungen, die weiter oben zitierte Aussage Schillebeeckx', „eine Wirklichkeit ist nicht zugleich zwei Wirklichkeiten" [EG 48], differenzierter zu fassen. Je nach Kontext kann man sagen, dass eine Wirklichkeit eine einzigartige niedrigere Entität mit ihren eigenen Gesetzmäßigkeiten und gleichzeitig Teil einer höheren Entität ist. Im Kontext des mystischen Leibes kann ein unabhängiger Mensch auch ein Glied am mystischen Christus sein. In der Eucharistie kann der Komplex an Atomen und Molekülen, aus dem das Brot besteht, seine eigene Seinsweise haben, auch wenn es der eucharistische Leib Christi wird. Im Augenblick der Wandlung wird das Brot durch Christus aufgehoben, sodass es sein eigentümliches Wesen als Brot beibehält und zugleich Teil seines eucharistischen Leibes wird. Wenn es vom Herrn aufgehoben wird, dann wird es in die Lage versetzt, die Seele des Kommunionempfängers zu nähren. Doch als Brot bleibt es weiterhin eine komplexe Struktur unbelebter Atome und Moleküle, die dazu geeignet ist, das leibliche Leben der Menschen zu ernähren.

So hat uns das neue Wissen der modernen Zeit dazu gezwungen, auf andere Weise als unsere Vorfahren früher zu sprechen. Wenn wir vom Wesen der Eucharistie sprechen, dann sagen wir, dass das Brot Teil Christi selbst wird. Wenn wir das gewöhnliche philosophische Wesen des eucharistischen Brotes unabhängig von seiner Funktion innerhalb der Eucharistiefeier betrachten, dann müssen wir sagen, dass es „wesenhaft" dasselbe bleibt wie vor der Konsekration. Doch sobald die Handlung vollzogen ist, ist seine höchste Eigenschaft die Fähigkeit, zum heiligenden Handeln Christi selbst beizutragen. Diese Zweideutigkeit im Hinblick auf die Bedeutung von „wesenhaft" ergibt sich, wenn man an die Funktion eines Neurons im menschlichen Gehirn denkt. An sich ist ein Neuron „wesenhaft" ein einzelliger Organismus. Doch zugleich trägt er kraft seines höheren Wesens zum menschlichen Denken und Begehren bei. Das verhält sich, wenn auch auf anderer Ebene, ebenso im Fall des eucharistischen Brotes. Der übernatürliche und wundersame Aspekt hierbei besteht darin, dass durch die Kraft des Geistes die höhere natürliche Wirklichkeit des Brotes etliche Ebenen der kosmischen Hierarchie überspringt, um die höchste von allen zu erreichen, nämlich die Ebene des inkarnierten Wortes.

Das ist eine Situation, die der des „mystischen Leibes" Christi ganz ähnlich ist. Wenn ein Bekehrter getauft wird, dann bekommt er Anteil an Christus. Und dennoch verändert er sein gewöhnliches philosophisches Wesen nicht. Was sein philosophisches Wesen betrifft, ist er immer noch ein Mensch, aber ein Mensch, der in einer so realen Weise mit Christus vereint ist, die nur mit den Worten des Apostels Paulus beschrieben werden kann, der sagt, dass nicht mehr er lebt, sondern dass Christus in ihm lebt (Gal 2,20). Was aber ist wichtiger: seine Teilhabe am mystischen Leib oder sein eigenes philosophisches Wesen? Ich denke, es ist wichtiger, dass er an Christus teilhat, und wenn man über sein Wesen im bedeutenderen Sinne des Wortes spricht, dann existiert er nicht länger als er selbst, sondern als Teil Christi. Das ist etwas, das im Sinne von Karl Rahners „übernatürlichem Existenzial" mit der gesamten Welt vor sich geht. Von Anfang an ist das „Wesen" der Welt ein übernatürliches, trotz der Tatsache, dass sie in sich immer noch ein bloß natürliches philosophisches Wesen hat.

Ist es falsch zu sagen, dass die Transsubstantiation das Brot der Messe in Christus selbst verwandelt, da doch das Brot zugleich Brot bleibt? Ich meine nein. Das ist kein Widerspruch. Was für ein Wunder die Eucharistie auch ist: Es ist kein Widerspruch, wenn man behauptet, dass die eucharistischen Gaben zwei „Wesen" haben. Vom zweiten, wundersamen Wesen könnte man aus einer bestimmten Perspektive sagen, dass es eher „akzidenziell" als „essenziell" sei. Doch dieser Sprachgebrauch ist unangemessen. Unsere gewöhnliche Art zu sprechen reicht nicht aus, um das Wesen der Eucharistie zum Ausdruck zu bringen.

Der Empfang der Eucharistie ist ein Mittel, durch das die menschlichen Glieder Christi vergöttlicht werden. Ohne ihres eigenen Wesens verlustig zu gehen werden sie seine Glieder. Wenn die Menschen im Himmel Vollkommenheit erlangen, dann werden sie ebenso rein und heilig sein, wie es das eucharistische Brot bereits ist. Die Parusie, die Wiederkunft Christi also, wird die Zeit sein, da das gesamte Universum Christus vollkommen unterworfen sein wird. Jetzt ist die gewöhnliche Materie zum Teil unter der Kontrolle sündiger Menschen und dämonischer Kräfte. Wenn die Sünde ausgetilgt sein wird und böse Kräfte aus der Welt vertrieben sein werden, dann wird das Universum selbst in vollem Sinne der kosmische Leib Christi und vollkommen seinen Wünschen und der Freiheit der Kinder Gottes, seiner Glieder, unterworfen sein. Der auferweckte physische Leib Christi ist ihm bereits unterworfen. Der Zustand, den wir nun für uns selbst herbeisehnen, ist der, in dem das gesamte Universum auf dieselbe Weise ihm unterworfen sein wird, einschließlich unseres eigenen Vernunftwesens und der niedrigeren Entitäten in uns, die nun zum Teil unabhängig von unserem Willen sind.

Die Lehre von der Eucharistie war für die Kirche des 16. Jahrhunderts ein Stolperstein. Die Konzilsväter wussten nichts von Molekülen oder Atomen noch von der empirischen Nachweisbarkeit ihrer Existenz im menschlichen Körper. Sie benutzten einfach die beste und klarste Sprache, die ihnen zu dieser Zeit zur Verfügung stand. Schillebeeckx hatte recht, wenn er sagte, dass sie einfach die ihnen von den Kirchenvätern überlieferte Lehre in der besten ihnen zur Verfügung stehenden Weise, das heißt mithilfe des thomasischen Begriffs der Transsubstantiation, wiederholten.

Die vom hl. Thomas bereitgestellte philosophische Theorie war gut für ihre Zeit, ja sogar gut für die Zeit des Trienter Konzils. Doch heute scheint sie angesichts der Erkenntnisse der modernen Naturwissenschaften unangemessen zu sein. Die Theorie der kosmischen Hierarchie, wie ich sie hier vorschlage, scheint besser geeignet zu sein. Sie zeigt, dass der Leib Christi während seines irdischen Daseins genauso wie unser Leib in sich Elementarteilchen, Atome, Moleküle, usw. enthielt. Jede dieser untergeordneten Entitäten verfügt über ihr eigenes aktuelles Dasein. Doch bei der Wandlung in der Messe werden sie von der Wirklichkeit Christi, der auf der rationalen und kosmischen Ebene existiert, aufgehoben.

Im *Katechismus der Katholischen Kirche* (Nr. 1374) wird das Konzil von Trient mit folgender Passage zitiert: „Im heiligsten Sakrament der Eucharistie ist wahrhaft, wirklich und substanzhaft [...] der ganze Christus enthalten." Dann zitiert er die Enzyklika Papst Pauls VI., in der es heißt, dass das Konzil von Trient sagen will, dass Jesu Gegenwart real im vollsten Sinne ist: „Diese Gegenwart wird nicht ausschlussweise ‚wirklich' genannt, [...] sondern vorzugsweise, weil sie substanziell ist; in ihr wird nämlich der ganze und unversehrte Christus, Gott und Mensch, gegenwärtig." (*Mysterium fidei*, 39)

Dies ist die Bedeutung der Worte des Tridentinums „Wahrhaft, wirklich und substanziell". Papst Paul VI. war kein Physiker. Er wiederholte einfach eine Lehre, die von den Kirchenvätern, von einer Zeit also, die nichts wusste von Molekülen und Atomen, zu uns gelangte.

Was ist nun die Bedeutung der „species" Brot und Wein, die nach Aussage des Tridentinums nach der Wandlung der Messe bleibt? Sie muss die Wirklichkeit von Brot und Wein sein, die durch den kosmischen Christus zum Realsymbol erhoben wurden, durch das er die Glieder der Kirche, seines mystischen Leibes, nährt.

III. DAS SAKRAMENTALE UNIVERSUM

Nachdem ich eine moderne Theorie der Transsubstantiation skizziert habe, bin ich nun in der Lage, deren Verhältnis zur Transsignifikation deutlicher zu sehen. Ich kann in einem qualifizierten Sinne der Behauptung Schoonenbergs zustimmen, dass „Transsubstantiation sich innerhalb einer Transsignifikation, einer Transfinalisation, vollzieht".[12] Wenn die eucharistischen *species* konsekriert werden, dann nehmen sie eine neue Bedeutung und eine neue Zielsetzung an, kraft derer sie als die symbolische Ursache der Einheit der Kirche und der Heiligung des einzelnen Kommunionempfängers fungieren können. Doch die Bedeutung, die sie annehmen, ist eine ganz besondere. Nun bezeichnen sie nicht nur die Einheit der Kirche, sondern auch die reale, ortsgebundene Gegenwart Christi, seine Verfügbarkeit „hier und jetzt" als ein Gegenstand der Anbetung und Quelle der Vergebung, Heilung und neuen Lebens im Geist. Sie könnten diese Bedeutung nicht wirklich besitzen, wenn der Herr nicht wirklich gegenwärtig wäre, wenn die eucharistischen *species* nicht bereits enthalten, was sie bezeichnen. Ebenso wenig könnte die Kirche eine sein oder könnten die Gläubigen in der machtvollen Weise geheiligt werden, wie es das Symbol intendiert, wenn dies nicht der Fall wäre. Die Transsubstantiation, das heißt die reale Gegenwart Christ selbst in den eucharistischen *species*, lässt Transsignifikation und Transfinalisation allererst echt werden.

Papst Paul VI. bestand in seiner Enzyklika aus dem Jahr 1965, *Mysterium fidei*, mit Recht darauf, dass der Gebrauch des Ausdrucks „Transsignifikation" eine Gefahr in sich berge, wenn nicht zugleich seine Verbindung mit „Transsubstantiation" deutlich gemacht wird. Die Eucharistie ist nicht nur ein Symbol, sondern auch eine kosmologische Wirklichkeit, etwas, was mit der zeitlichen, räumlichen und materiellen Welt zu tun hat, in der wir leben. Die moderne Philosophie ist zum Teil nicht in der Lage, diesem kosmologischen Aspekt das nötige Gewicht beizumessen. Hierfür brauchen wir eine Kosmologie, die die subjektive Perspektive nicht nur mit der objektiveren und empirischen der Naturwissenschaften verbindet, sondern auch mit der traditionellen Lehre der Kirche.

„Die Redeweise von der Transsubstantiation [...] betont die Tatsache, dass das Ganze der Schöpfung letztlich sakramental ist, das heißt es hat innerhalb der göttlichen Schöpfungsordnung die Fähigkeit, das Handeln zu inkarnieren, in dem Gott dem Menschen sein Leben gibt" (Powers 1967, 185–86). Weil die Materie für sich genommen eine potenziell sakramentale Wirklichkeit ist, kann die dem Logos eignende Macht, sich selbst zu inkarnieren über seinen unmittelbaren persönlichen Leib hinaus wirksam werden, um die eucharistischen Gaben Brot und Wein und durch sie die anbetende Gemeinde zu verwandeln. Letztlich wird diese Macht die gesamte Welt verwandeln. So spricht der heilige Paulus in seinem Brief an die Römer davon, wie die Schöpfung selbst von ihrer Preisgabe an den Verfall befreit werden und die Freiheit der Herrlichkeit der Kinder Gottes erlangen wird. „Wir wissen, dass die ganze Schöpfung bis jetzt in Geburtswehen stöhnt. Und nicht nur die Schöpfung, sondern wir selbst, die die ersten Früchte des Geistes haben, stöhnen in unserem Inneren und warten darauf, dass wir an Kindes statt angenommen und unser Leib erlöst wird" (Röm. 8,21–23) Die Verwandlung der Schöpfung, die in einigen Menschen bereits teilweise vollzogen wurde, wird letztlich die Welt umfangen. Als der kosmische Leib des Logos selbst wird sie die verwandelnde Kraft seiner Auferstehung erfahren und wenn nicht Teil des „mystischen Leibes" im strengen Sinne, so doch wenigstens mit ihm so verbunden sein, dass sie an der „Herrlichkeit der Kinder Gottes" teilhat. Das Zeichen und die Verheißung dieser letztlichen, eschatologischen Verwandlung ist die Verwandlung der eucharistischen Gaben Brot und Wein.

Niemand hat dies schöner zum Ausdruck gebracht als Pierre Teilhard de Chardin in verschiedenen seiner kurzen Aufsätze. In *Die Messe über die Welt* lud er den Herrn ein, ihn zu ermächtigen, die Wandlungsworte „Dies ist mein Leib ... dies ist mein Blut" über der Schöpfung auszusprechen.[13] In einem anderen Aufsatz gibt er die Erfahrung eines nicht genannten Freundes – wahrscheinlich handelt es sich um ihn selbst – wieder, den, als er vor der Monstranz kniete, „ein ganz eigenartiger Eindruck überkam" (Teilhard de Chardin 1994, 54). Als er schaute und betete, begann sich die Hostie in der Monstranz vor ihm nach und nach auszudehnen, bis sie die ganze Welt umfasste und in sich im Maße des Möglichen die Substanz aller Dinge aufnahm.

Teilhard de Chardin scheint uns eine Einsicht vermittelt zu haben, die ihm für unser wissenschaftliches Zeitalter gegeben wurde. Das Universum, das die Naturwissenschaftler analysieren und deren Struktur sie in gewisser Hinsicht in einem Ausmaß offengelegt haben, das sich frühere Zeiten nicht erträumt hätten, wird zutiefst von der Eucharistie her verstanden. Es ist wirklich der kosmische Leib Christi, eine Wirklichkeit, die dazu bestimmt ist, dadurch verherrlicht zu werden, dass sie zur Eucharistie wird bzw. die Transsubstantiation an sich erfährt. Deshalb ist die Geschichte des Universums eine Art Eucharistie, eine kosmische Liturgie. Die als Opfergabe dargebotene Materie wurde bei der Schöpfung bereitet und den Geschöpfen als den Priestern übereignet, damit sie dem Vater als Opfergabe dargebracht werde. Aufgrund der Sünde wurde das Opfer nicht vollzogen, bis schließlich, als die Zeit erfüllt war, der wahre Hohepriester kam und „ein für allemal das Heiligtum betrat, nicht mit dem Blut von Böcken und Kälbern, sondern mit seinem eigenen Blut, und so die ewige Erlösung erwirkte" (Hebr 9,12). Durch und im Opfer Jesu wurde das ganze materiell-spirituelle Universum als Opfer dargebracht und zum Teil verwandelt. Bis jetzt hat die verwandelnde Kraft dieses Opfers ihr Werk noch nicht vollendet, da wir unsere eigene Einwilligung in das Opfer noch nicht vollständig vollzogen haben. Doch wir erwarten den Tag, an dem unser Opfer vollständig sein wird und der, dem es dargebracht wird, alle Dinge neu machen wird (Offb 21,5). Die Schöpfung wird erneuert in Jesus, denn ihre tiefste Wirklichkeit besteht darin, dass sie der kosmische Leib ist, der letztlich an seiner persönlichen Verherrlichung teilhaben muss.

Zurzeit ist es ein Erfordernis der ökologischen Krise, dass wir den kosmischen Aspekt der eucharistischen Symbolik besonders betonen. Im Wissen darum, dass die Erde und das Universum ihre Einheit und tiefste Wirklichkeit in Christus haben, müssen wir lernen, deren Unversehrtheit zu respektieren und danach streben, die Sachwalter und Priester und nicht die Ausbeuter der Schöpfung zu werden. Wenn wir das eucharistische Brot essen, dann stärken wir unser Gespür für die Abhängigkeit von der Welt und unsere Einheit mit ihr. Die Eucharistie ist ein sakramentales Symbol dafür, dass Christus sein Leben mit uns teilt, was unserer tiefsten Verehrung würdig ist.

Dieser Vollzug befähigt uns, unser modernes naturwissenschaftliches Wissen in eine umfassendere Perspektive einzuordnen. Die Naturwissenschaft ist eine wunderbare Gabe Gottes, doch sie erfüllt ihren Zweck nicht, für den sie uns von Gott verliehen wurde, wenn sie nicht in die höhere Weisheit integriert wird, die nur dann gegeben ist, wenn wir die „Messe über die Welt" feiern. Wenn unsere im Entstehen begriffene planetarische Zivilisation lernt, diese Messe darzubringen, wird die reduktionistische Verhärtung, die der ausschließlichen Konzentration auf die mechanischen Seiten der Welt geschuldet ist, gelöst, und wir werden offen für eine menschlichere Haltung.

Dies wird sich auf unser Verständnis von der Bedeutung und dem Zweck der Zwillingsschwester der Wissenschaft, nämlich der Technologie, und auf die modernen Techniken auswirken, die den Geist der Technik auf das gesellschaftliche und wirtschaftliche Leben der Menschheit ausdehnen. Die Schaffung und der Gebrauch von Mechanismen werden in ihrer Hinordnung auf die integrierte Ganzheit des menschlichen Lebens und der ganzen Schöpfung im Logos und als ein wertvoller Dienst an Zielen und Bemühungen gesehen werden, die weit über den Bereich des bloß Technologischen hinausgehen. Der Mythos der Maschine, die Verherrlichung der Mechanik um ihrer selbst willen, wird einem Ideal des Dienstes und der Verehrung, dem kosmischen *opus Dei*, weichen, in dem materielle, soziale und wirtschaftliche Techniken die Sehnsucht nach Spiritualität und göttlicher Herrlichkeit fördern und ermöglichen.

Translated by Dr. Bruno Kern, Mainz, Germany

ANMERKUNGEN

1. Heinrich Denzinger, *Kompendium der Glaubensbekenntnisse und kirchlichen Lehrentscheidungen: Verbessert, erweitert, ins Deutsche übertragen und unter Mitarbeit von Helmut Hoping herausgegeben von Peter Hünermann* (Lateinisch und Deutsch), 43rd ed. (Freiburg i. Br.: Herder, 2010), Nr. 1652.

2. Edward Schillebeeckx, *Die eucharistische Gegenwart* [= EG]: *Zur Diskussion über die Realpräsenz*, 2nd ed. (Düsseldorf: Patmos, 1968), 34–49.

3. Piet Schoonenberg, „Inwieweit ist die Lehre von der Transsubstantiation historisch bestimmt?," [= T] *Concilium* 3/4 (April 1967), 305–11, hier 30.

4. William B. Ashworth Jr., "Catholicism and Early Modern Science," *God and Nature*, ed. David C. Lindberg and Ronald L. Numbers (Berkeley: University of California Press, 1986), chap. 5, p. 151. Also Frederick Copleston, *A History of Philosophy*, 9 vols. (New York: Doubleday, 1985), 4:126–28.

5. Joseph M. Powers, *Eucharistic Theology* (New York: Herder & Herder, 1967), 166.

6. Robert J. Russell, William R. Stoeger, and George V. Coyne, eds., *Physics, Philosophy, and Theology* (Vatican City: Vatican Observatory, 1988 [distributed except in Italy and Vatican City by University of Notre Dame Press]), M1–M14.

7. Kol. 1,15–20; Eph. 1,9–10; 20–23 und Röm. 8,19–23. Neben diesen Versen haben auch Joh. 1,1–5 und Hebr. 1,3 -4 sowie 1 Kor. 8,6 und Phil. 2,6–11 eine ähnliche kosmische Bedeutung.

8. David Noel Freedman, ed., *The Anchor Bible Dictionary*, 6 vols. (New York: Doubleday, 1992), 1:771.

9. François Jacob, *The Logic of Life: A History of Heredity* (New York: Pantheon, 1973), 302; zit. bei Ernst Mayr, *This Is Biology: The Science of the Living World* (Cambridge, MA: Belknap Press of Harvard University Press, 1997), 19.

10. Michael Polanyi, *Implizites Wissen* (Frankfurt a. M.: Suhrkamp, 1985), 38–39. Polanyi's Analogie beweist natürlich seinen Standpunkt nicht, veranschaulicht ihn aber.

11. Bernard Lonergan, *Methode in der Theologie* (Leipzig: St. Benno, 1991), 340.

12. Powers, *Eucharistic Theology*, 173.

13. Pierre Teilhard de Chardin, *Lobgesang des Alls* (Olten: Walter-Verlag, 1964), 19.

LA MISA SOBRE EL MUNDO

I. Theología eucarística y cosmología
II. Transubstanciación
III. El universo sacramental
    Notas

La Misa sobre el Mundo

El presente artículo tiene tres secciones. La primera se refiere a la relación entre la teoría teológica de la transubstanciación y la de la *transignificación* (cambio de significado) y *transfinalización* (cambio de finalidad o propósito), ideas que fueron introducidas justo antes del Vaticano II por teólogos del norte de Europa. La segunda sección desarrolla una visión holística de la naturaleza de la materia. Nuestro conocimiento científico actual parece requerir que abandonemos la teoría aristotélica del hilemorfismo a favor de una teoría en la cual los seres reales de un cierto nivel 'subliman' seres reales, pero subordinados, de niveles inferiores. Por ejemplo, un ser humano es una sustancia que incluye dentro de sí muchas substancias menores. Cuando estaba encarnado, el cuerpo físico de Cristo incluía dentro de sí un gran número de átomos y moléculas interconectadas. La tercera sección discute ideas de Teilhard de Chardin sobre la relación de Cristo con la materia.

I. Teología eucarística y cosmología

En el siglo XVI el Concilio de Trento estableció la enseñanza de la Iglesia sobre la Eucaristía en una forma que parecía presuponer un punto de vista conceptual aristotélico-tomista.

> Si alguien dice que en el santo sacramento de la Eucaristía la sustancia del pan y del vino permanecen junto con el cuerpo y la sangre de nuestro Señor Jesucristo y niega esa transformación única y maravillosa de la

sustancia completa del pan en Su cuerpo y de la sustancia completa del vino en Su sangre mientras sólo las especies de pan y vino permanecen, transformación que la Iglesia Católica muy acertadamente llama transubstanciación, *anatema sit*.[1]

La forma más fácil y clara de comprender esta enseñanza es a través de la doctrina escolástica de sustancia y accidentes. Según Aristóteles, los accidentes existen en y a través de las sustancias, calificándolas de distintas maneras. Santo Tomás sugirió que en la Eucaristía tenemos un caso único en el cual la sustancia es transformada en otra sin que los accidentes de la primera perezcan. Por el poder milagroso de Dios los accidentes del pan y el vino permanecen aún después de que la sustancia a la cual estaban adheridos haya desaparecido. Cómo podía ser esto era, por supuesto, muy difícil de ver, pero en realidad nadie esperaba ser capaz de comprender la Eucaristía completamente.

Sin embargo, de hecho el decreto del Concilio de Trento no usó el término aristotélico de 'accidentes', sino más bien empleó el latino 'especies', un término más ambiguo que podía tener un significado objetivo como 'accidentes' o uno subjetivo como 'apariencias'. Si las especies son objetivas, como los accidentes aristotélicos, o son más como las apariencias subjetivas, no es inmediatamente evidente.

¿Podemos tomar esto como una indicación de que Trento fue cauteloso y no quiso refrendar el aristotelismo ni ninguna otra teoría filosófica y, por tanto, no sólo 'especies' sino también 'sustancia' debe ser interpretado en un sentido general muy amplio? Escribiendo poco después del Concilio Vaticano II, E. Schillebeeckx sostuvo que esta es la opinión de la mayoría de los historiadores modernos del Concilio de Trento.[2] Sin embargo, su opinión era más compleja. Desde su punto de vista, mientras es verdad que Trento no quiso canonizar el aristotelismo, el pensamiento de los Padres del Concilio estaba necesariamente ligado al sistema conceptual aristotélico en el cual la mayoría de ellos habían sido entrenados. Sólo usando las categorías del aristotelianismo estaban ellos en capacidad de expresar su fe en la presencia real de Cristo en la Eucaristía.

En un artículo en 1967, Schoonenberg, colega holandés de Schillebeeckx, decía más o menos lo mismo: 'Esto muestra que la declaración de fe hecha por un concilio o por cualquiera nunca puede ser satisfactoriamente separada del pensamiento teológico del momento, y ciertamente no por los mismos que han hecho la declaración. Pero nosotros, en una época posterior, *podemos* desprender la formulación de un credo de sus circunstancias históricas'.[3]

La distinción entre una verdad dogmática fundamental y su formulación se aprecia en la historia de la doctrina de la Eucaristía anterior a Trento. De acuerdo con Schillebeeckx, se pueden distinguir tres niveles en la enseñanza sobre la Eucaristía de Tomás de Aquino en el siglo XIII: (1) el nivel de *fe* en la presencia real, (2) el nivel en el cual se afirma un cambio real *ontológico* en las especies de la Eucaristía, y (3) el nivel en el cual este cambio ontológico se expresa en términos de las categorías aristotélicas (E 63). Schillebeeckx sostenía que hoy las categorías aristotélicas pueden verse como inadecuadas y por tanto las enseñanzas de Aquino deben ser puestas de lado. Pero ¿qué pasa con el nivel ontológico? La creencia en una transformación ontológica en el pan y el vino eucarísticos se remonta hasta los Padres griegos de la Iglesia. Como decía Schillebeeckx, ellos no pensaban en la sustancia en términos aristotélicos sino en términos de un ser independiente o realidad fundamental. La manera en que el Logos toma posesión de los elementos eucarísticos era, para ellos, comparable a la manera en la cual él primero tomó posesión de su cuerpo en el vientre de su madre, la Virgen María. Ambos eventos tuvieron lugar por el poder del Espíritu Santo. Por tanto, para ellos, en la Eucaristía el pan y el vino pierden su realidad independiente, o sustancia, y se convierten en el cuerpo y la sangre de Cristo. La fe Patrística fundamental era la misma que la de Trento pero expresada en categorías diferentes, no aristotélicas. Hay un cambio ontológico real en los elementos eucarísticos y es este cambio el que le da su carácter especial a la Eucaristía. Hay, pues, un significado básico no-aristotélico de 'sustancia' en la tradición que llevó a Trento.

> Era esencial y fundamental al dogma de fe que no hubiera *realidad* de pan después de la consagración, ya que, si la definitiva *realidad* presente en la Eucaristía debiera llamarse pan, habría simplemente pan (¡una realidad no puede al mismo tiempo ser dos realidades!) y la presencia eucarística sólo se podría concebir simbólicamente . . .

. . . Fue únicamente en un intento de explicar 'la permanencia de las especies' que la teoría de sustancia y accidentes surgió en las mentes de los padres del Concilio, con el resultado de que, hablando tradicionalmente de 'sustancia' de pan, inevitablemente produjeron un contraste entre sustancia y accidentes.(E 74–75)

Por tanto, aun cuando su formulación aristotélica puede no ser tomada en cuenta, la comprensión de Trento de la presencia eucarística no sólo afirma su realidad sino que también requiere un cambio ontológico en los elementos eucarísticos. 'En otras palabras, la presencia de un *aspecto ontológico* en el reparto *sacramental* del pan es sin duda un dato de fe y no simplemente un aspecto de 'fraseología" (E 81–82). Así Schillebeeckx concluía que Trento no tiene que ser interpretado en categorías aristotélico-tomista. Sin embargo, él sí creía que tiene que haber un cambio ontológico en relación a los elementos eucarísticos, de la misma manera que en la mente de los Padres de la Iglesia tenía que haber un cambio ontológico en relación con la formación del cuerpo de Cristo en el vientre de la Virgen María.

La relación entre la Eucaristía y las teorías cosmológicas siguieron siendo un problema para la ortodoxia católica mucho después de Trento. La escuela dominante del pensamiento de la Contrarreforma interpretó el dogma básico en términos de la teoría aristotélico-tomista del hilemorfismo, relativamente clara (aunque al mismo tiempo desconcertante), y, en una época de violentas polémicas religiosas, no estaba inclinada a ser tolerante con otras alternativas. Así, en 1663 las *Meditaciones* de Descartes fueron colocadas en el Index Romano de libros prohibidos porque su comprensión de materia se estimaba incompatible con la doctrina eucarística.[4] Nuestro siglo, por supuesto, es menos ingenuo en relación con teorías teológicas y científicas que lo que fue el siglo XVI. Tampoco exigimos tanta integración entre la física y la teología como las épocas anteriores lo hicieron. Sin embargo, el mismo problema básico ha reaparecido en nuestro tiempo. Schillebeeckx escribe:

Ya estaba claro, en el período entre las dos guerras mundiales, que la transubstanciación necesitaba interpretación. Los datos de la física

moderna habían estremecido hasta sus fundamentos a las especulacio-
nes neo-escolásticas sobre el concepto de sustancia. . . .

. . . Entre las dos guerras mundiales aparecieron un número casi
incalculable de libros y artículos relativos al impacto de las ciencias
positivas sobre la comprensión tradicional de la Eucaristía . . .

. . . Porque los teólogos que trataban de vincular los descubrimientos
de esta nueva ciencia al concepto de transubstanciación llegaron a con-
clusiones que no ofrecían perspectivas y porque su punto de partida era
que un cambio ontológico no podía dejar la realidad física intacta, ellos
mismos, más que nadie, contribuyeron al punto de vista de que una
comprensión de la Eucaristía en términos de la filosofía natural era
insostenible. (E 94–96)

Esta creencia, cada vez mayor, fue uno de los factores que llevó a la
adopción de un enfoque más personalista por parte de los teólogos del
norte de Europa después de la II Guerra Mundial. Otro factor fueron los
desarrollos contemporáneos en filosofía que permitieron nuevas categorías que parecían mejor adaptadas para expresar la naturaleza humana y
simbólica de los sacramentos en general y de la Eucaristía en particular. El
pensamiento existencialista, fenomenológico y hermenéutico no opera
en el modo óntico adecuado a las ciencias, sino dentro de un horizonte
fundamentalmente determinado por la experiencia humana subjetiva, la
autoexpresión personal y simbólica y la comunicación interpersonal. Dentro de este horizonte la acción de Cristo en la Eucaristía es vista más en
términos de significado y autoexpresión simbólica que en los conceptos,
más objetivos y cosmológicos, del neoescolasticismo. Como resultado, el
cambio en los elementos eucarísticos de pan y vino que tiene lugar durante
la misa, en la consagración, se entiende más como un cambio de significado y propósito que de sustancia. Por ello los términos 'transignificación' (cambio de significado) y 'transfinalización' (cambio de finalidad)
toman la delantera ante la tradicional 'transubstanciación' (cambio de
sustancia).

Sin embargo, hay dificultades en relación con este enfoque antropológico. En 1965, el papa Pablo VI emitió su encíclica *Mysterium Fidei*.
Entre las opiniones con las que discrepó fue con la pretensión de que el
cambio de significado o finalidad de los elementos eucarísticos, implicado

en el papel que juegan en la acción simbólica y sacramental de la misa, proporciona una explicación adecuada de transubstanciación. En su opinión la tradición autorizada de la Iglesia muestra que hay un cambio ontológico en las especies consagradas que va más allá de lo que se puede expresar en términos de significado y simbolismo. El término tradicional transubstanciación expresa esto y no puede ser dejado de lado en favor de la transignificación o la transfinalización.

Schillebeeckx y Schoonenberg respondieron en formas diferentes a tales observaciones críticas relativas a transignificación. Comentando *Mysterium Fidei*, el segundo distingue entre dos tipos de señales-de-acción:

> Hay señales-de-acción que traen algo a nuestro conocimiento, y por tanto llevan a un conocimiento, provocan sentimientos o transmiten órdenes (en relación con estos últimos piense en las señales de tránsito). Pero también hay señales-de-acción—y aquí la *acción* es de fundamental importancia—en las que lo que se muestra al mismo tiempo se comunica o por lo menos se ofrece. El contenido de este segundo tipo de señales-de-acción es siempre una forma de amor o comunión—darse la mano, un beso, etc. Este segundo tipo merece plenamente el calificativo de 'señal efectiva', aunque el primer tipo es también efectivo en algún grado en cuanto comunica conocimiento y por tanto también establece algún tipo de comunión, aunque sólo implícitamente. Podemos por tanto hablar de signos 'informativos' por una parte y signos 'comunicativos' por la otra. (T 88)

De acuerdo con Schoonenberg, *Mysterium Fidei* tenía en mente sólo signos-de- información cuando negó que la transubstanciación de las especies eucarísticas pudiera ser representada en términos de transignificación. Pero la Eucaristía es un signo de comunicación 'en el cual el Señor entrega su cuerpo para convertirnos en su cuerpo y en el cual se entrega a sí mismo a nosotros para comunión en y con el' (T 90).

Schillebeeckx respondió en forma diferente. Aunque estaba de acuerdo con Schoonenberg y con el teólogo inglés Charles Davis sobre la importancia y la utilidad del enfoque antropológico para entender la Eucaristía, sin embargo preguntaba '¿es la transignificación idéntica a la transubstanciación, o será una consecuencia o una implicación de la transubstanciación? La cuestión que surge aquí en toda su amplitud es la de la realidad' (E 145). Su respuesta fue: 'Varios autores modernos correctamente consideran la creación, el comienzo de la alianza de gracia, también como el telón de fondo del evento eucarístico' (E 127). Percibiendo la tradición de la Iglesia a la luz de ese principio él no podía

> estar satisfecho personalmente con una interpretación *puramente* fenomenológica sin densidad metafísica. La realidad no es obra del hombre—en este sentido, realismo es esencial a la fe cristiana. En mi reinterpretación del dato tridentino, entonces, no puedo permanecer contento simplemente con una apelación a un *sólo dar sentido* humano, aunque esto se sitúe dentro de la fe. Por supuesto una transignificación de este tipo tiene un lugar en la Eucaristía, pero es sostenida y evocada por la actividad recreativa del Espíritu Santo, el Espíritu de Cristo enviado por el Padre. Dios mismo *actúa* en la esfera de la Iglesia activamente creyente, actuante y celebrante, y el resultado de esta actividad divina salvadora es sacramentalmente una 'nueva creación' que perpetúa y ahonda nuestra relación escatológica con el reino de Dios. (E 150–51)

Al decir que 'la realidad no es obra del hombre' Schillebeeckx puso su dedo en una debilidad vital en el intento de explicar la Eucaristía completamente en los términos de transignificación. Cuando un joven le da a su novia una sortija su acción simbólica cambia la situación humana en una forma muy importante.[5] Pero esto no afecta la naturaleza física de la sortija. Uno podría tal vez decir que sí cambia la 'realidad relacional' de la sortija, pero ese cambio no es capaz de expresar el sentido de la tradición de la Iglesia sobre la Eucaristía. El Cristo glorificado se puede entregar a sí mismo con una completitud y un poder que no le es posible a los seres humanos ordinarios, y, como dice Schillebeeckx, su auto donación eucarística es un don de sí mismo, no de sí en una dádiva (E 138–39). La analogía entre la entrega de regalos humanos y el don de sí de Cristo en la Eucaristía es demasiado remota y demasiado débil para que pueda tener un poder explicativo adecuado.

Schoonenberg está evadiendo la necesidad de construir una cosmología que tome seriamente nuestro moderno conocimiento científico de la materia y que también proporcione categorías en función de las cuales la transubstanciación pudiera ser entendida. La pretensión de que un objeto material es transubstanciado pura y simplemente por asumir un papel en una acción-signo es demasiado débil. La insatisfacción expresada en *Mysterium Fidei* no es sin fundamento. Aun cuando la cosmología aristotélica-escolástica es inadecuada, la doctrina de la transubstanciación continúa expresando la preocupación de la Iglesia acerca de la realidad de la materia y de la contribución real que, hasta en el nivel espiritual, la materia hace a la existencia. Si la materia es sublimada en ideas, la realidad espiritual misma eventualmente se va a evaporar en ilusiones y deseos piadosos.

La conclusión de Schillebeeckx de que la transignificación no es equivalente o idéntica a la transubstanciación es indiscutiblemente correcta. Sin embargo, no llega muy lejos explicando el 'cómo' de la presencia eucarística aun cuando sí insiste en que es sin duda inseparable de ella (E 155–56). En la Edad Media el problema de la relación entre la teología eucarística y la cosmología era inevitable al igual que insoluble, en vista de la suposición generalizada de que la teoría del hilemorfismo es correcta. Ahora, sin embargo, tenemos disponible una teoría diferente sobre la materia. En nuestra época la teología no puede evitar tomar en cuenta a la ciencia y, como Juan Pablo II ha insistido, tenemos que aprender a manejar eso.[6] Dejar de integrar consideraciones cosmológicas en la propia teología la convierte en etérea o idealista. No podemos simplemente olvidar lo que conocemos acerca de la estructura de la materia.

Me parece que hoy el estado de la cuestión sobre la transubstanciación es esencialmente la misma que Pablo VI, Schillebeeckx y Schoonenberg nos dejaron en los años 60. Los teólogos han tornado su atención a otros varios aspectos de la Eucaristía pero la intrigante pregunta que se presentó entonces aún permanece. Yo supongo que una razón para esto es porque la mayoría de los teólogos evitan pensar sobre cuestiones científicas y la mayoría de los científicos evitan las teológicas. Pero en cualquier caso, yo me aboco ahora a la tarea de desarrollar una relación moderna satisfactoria de la transubstanciación.

II. Transubstanciación

El nuevo testamento emplea el término 'cuerpo' con referencia a Cristo por lo menos en tres formas diferentes: Jesús es un hombre y por tanto tiene un cuerpo físico. Está íntimamente unido e identificado con la Iglesia y por tanto él tiene también un cuerpo místico. Al recibir la Eucaristía nosotros comemos su cuerpo y por tanto él tiene un cuerpo eucarístico. Adicionalmente con probabilidad hay un cuarto cuerpo al que se refiere el Nuevo Testamento. Teilhard de Chardin encontró inspiración en varios pasajes famosos de San Pablo que hablan de la estatura cósmica y el papel de Cristo.[7] Uno de ellos es Colosenses 1:15–20, el cual probablemente es una adaptación de un himno cristiano de los primeros tiempos que exaltaba el señorío de Cristo sobre toda la creación. Este himno parece haber sostenido que él es la cabeza del cuerpo, refiriéndose, en este contexto, al cuerpo cósmico destacado en el pensamiento helenístico.[8] En el texto canónico de Colosenses el autor ha cambiado la referencia al 'cuerpo' por la Iglesia. Sin embargo, parecería que esto no cambia la comprensión general en Colosenses de la relación entre Cristo y el cosmos, que yo expreso aquí diciendo que él tiene un 'cuerpo cósmico' para distinguirlo de su 'cuerpo místico', la Iglesia.

Estos cuatro cuerpos de Cristo están, por supuesto, estrechamente vinculados. Yo expreso esto diciendo que son 'inadecuadamente distintos'. Su distinción no les impide constituir una única realidad, porque son aspectos de la realidad comprehensiva del Logos encarnado. Como veremos, cada cuerpo ejemplifica un patrón común que es verificado en cada caso de forma algo diferente.

Creo que para comprender esto primero debe uno comprender lo que llamo 'la jerarquía cósmica'. La ciencia natural moderna ha descubierto dentro de los seres humanos una jerarquía de entidades menores, o sea, organismos, órganos y tejidos, células, moléculas, átomos, nucleones, electrones y quarks, y actualmente se cuestiona sobre otros aún más pequeños. Así, todas las entidades en la jerarquía (en cualquiera de los niveles menos en el más bajo) están compuestas de una o más entidades subordinadas que provienen de los niveles inferiores.

Una pregunta crucial es si una entidad dada puede o no ser 'reducida' a las entidades dentro de ella. ¿Qué tipos de entidades pueden ser reducidas, sin que quede nada, a aquellas en un nivel más bajo y cuáles, si es que hay, no se pueden reducir? Cuando uno dice que una entidad particular es irreducible, uno quiere decir que esa entidad posee propiedades únicas 'de nivel más alto' que no pueden ser explicadas en términos de las entidades subordinadas dentro de ella. Estas entidades inferiores contribuyen a las propiedades de la entidad superior, pero esta última tiene algo más. En sus acciones muestra una calidad superior –y en los niveles más altos una conciencia unificada- que nunca se podrá explicar por las entidades subordinadas dentro de ella. Por otra parte, si una entidad es reducible, entonces puede ser explicada enteramente en términos de las entidades inferiores. En este caso, la acción supuestamente unificada de la entidad superior se debe enteramente a la interacción de las entidades más pequeñas.

En nuestro actual contexto teológico podemos asumir que las entidades racionales como nosotros no pueden ser reducidos a niveles inferiores. Ciertamente espero que la mayoría de los lectores estarán de acuerdo con mi aseveración de que hay una cantidad de niveles irreducibles en la jerarquía natural. Creo que estos incluyen, por lo menos, los niveles de inanimados, animados, sentientes y racionales, así como el nivel cósmico, cuya única entidad es el Cristo cósmico. En mi opinión también hay otro, el nivel más bajo y por ahora desconocido, el elemental inanimado. Es muy posible que haya más, pero para nuestro propósito es suficiente considerar sólo los seis que he mencionado. La entidad en un nivel dado tiene una propiedad esencial que no posee ninguno de los de órdenes inferiores. Así, ni una entidad racional como el ser humano ni una entidad sentiente como un perro puede ser explicado completamente en términos de sus componentes. Las entidades más pequeñas del nivel inanimado más bajo son, por supuesto, irreducibles. Son los átomos de los griegos antiguos, de lo que todo lo demás ha sido hecho. Yo los llamo 'entidades elementales'. Hoy día las entidades irreducibles de cualquier nivel son con frecuencia llamados *holones* o *integrones*.[9]

Antes del período moderno se creía que el universo era estático y que, después de un pequeño período de creación divina, siempre ha tenido el mismo tipo de estructura jerárquica que yo he descrito. Supuestamente la historia comenzó con el Hombre. Pero en el siglo XIX se dieron cuenta de que el universo entero tiene una historia. En el siglo XX el descubrimiento del 'Big Bang', como se le llamó, puso de manifiesto que la jerarquía cósmica que he descrito es el resultado de un desarrollo gigantesco. El universo comenzó con sólo una clase de holones elementales y entonces los superiores se desarrollaron uno por uno, terminando en época comparativamente reciente con la aparición del Hombre. La evolución es la historia del desarrollo progresivo de la jerarquía cósmica.

La naturaleza racional del Hombre depende de todo tipo de entidades inferiores en la jerarquía cósmica. Los procesos sensoriales, que son muy parecidos a los ejercitados por otros animales superiores, apoyan nuestro pensamiento racional. Estos procesos sensoriales a su vez están apoyados por procesos vitales de neuronas y otras células que a su vez se apoyan en los procesos, aún más fundamentales, de la materia inanimada. Las entidades sensoriales, vitales e inanimadas envueltas en los procesos humanos tienen su propia independencia. Las entidades en los niveles inferiores han sido adaptadas a los superiores, pero esencialmente son iguales a las poseídas por entidades similares que son independientes del Hombre. El corazón de un cochino puede ocupar el lugar de un corazón humano, un aparato mecánico una rodilla. Michael Polanyi ha descrito la situación comparándola con el habla humana:

> Incluye cinco niveles; a saber, la producción (1) de voz, (2) de palabras, (3) de oraciones, (4) de estilo, y (5) de composición literaria. Cada uno de estos niveles está sujeto a sus propias leyes, según está prescrito (1) por la fonética, (2) por la lexicografía, (3) por la gramática, (4) por la estilística, y (5) por la crítica literaria. Estos niveles forman una jerarquía de entidades comprensivas, pues los principios de cada nivel operan bajo el control del siguiente nivel superior. La voz que se produce está conformada en palabras por un vocabulario; un vocabulario dado se conforma en oraciones de acuerdo con la gramática; y las oraciones se puede hacer que se acomoden a un estilo que, a su vez, puede transmitir las ideas de una composición literaria. Así, cada nivel está sometido a

un doble control; primero por las leyes que se aplican a sus elementos mismos y en segundo lugar por las leyes que controlan la entidad comprensiva que ellos forman.

Por tanto, la operación de un nivel superior no puede ser explicada por las leyes que gobiernan sus componentes particulares que forman el nivel inferior. No se puede derivar un vocabulario de la fonética; no se puede derivar del vocabulario la gramática de un lenguaje; un uso correcto de la gramática no da lugar a un buen estilo; y el buen estilo no convierte al contenido en una pieza de prosa. Podemos concluir entonces en forma general . . . que es imposible representar los principios que organizan el nivel superior por las leyes que gobiernan sus particulares aislados.[10]

Cada nivel independiente tiene sus propias leyes, pero al mismo tiempo está adaptado al nivel superior encima de sí. Podemos aplicar esto a la situación presente y hablar de 'sublimación'. Sublimación es un término hegeliano original que es frecuentemente usado por los teólogos modernos para decir que

lo que sublima va más allá de lo que es sublimado, introduce algo nuevo y distinto, pone todo sobre una nueva base, y sin embargo, lejos de interferir con lo que es sublimado o destruirlo, al contrario lo necesita, lo incluye, preserva todas sus características y propiedades propias y las lleva adelante a una realización más completa dentro de un contexto más rico.[11]

Yo estoy aplicando la palabra a la cosmología y sostengo que en una jerarquía cósmica las entidades superiores subliman a las inferiores. Sabemos que el cuerpo místico de Cristo sublima los seres humanos para que sean sus miembros. Por tanto se convierten en algo mayor de lo que son en sí mismos. Similarmente, en la Eucaristía, él sublima la materia del pan y del vino de modo que, conservando sus 'propias características y propiedades' son llevados 'hacia una realización mayor dentro de un contexto más rico' de su cuerpo cósmico.

Así estamos obligados a distinguir la afirmación de Schillebeeckx que citamos arriba de que 'una realidad no puede ser al mismo tiempo dos realidades' (E 74–75). Se podría decir, dependiendo del contexto, que una realidad es tanto una única entidad inferior que posee sus propias leyes como, al mismo tiempo, parte de una superior. En el cuerpo místico, un ser humano independiente puede también ser miembro del cuerpo místico de Cristo. En la Eucaristía el complejo de átomos y moléculas que constituye el pan puede tener su propio modo de ser aun cuando se convierte también en el cuerpo eucarístico de Cristo. En el momento de la consagración el pan es sublimado por Cristo de modo que, aún reteniendo su propia esencia de pan, se vuelve parte del cuerpo eucarístico de Cristo. Cuando es sublimado por el Señor se vuelve capaz de alimentar el alma del comulgante. Sin embargo, como pan, continúa siendo una estructura compleja de átomos y moléculas inanimados apropiada para alimentar la vida corporal de los seres humanos.

Así el nuevo conocimiento de la era moderna nos ha forzado a hablar en forma diferente a como nuestros antecesores lo hicieron en épocas anteriores. Cuando hablamos de la naturaleza de la Eucaristía decimos que el pan se vuelve parte de Cristo mismo. Si estamos considerando la naturaleza filosófica ordinaria del pan eucarístico aparte de su función en la Eucaristía, tendríamos que decir que permanece 'esencialmente' el mismo que antes de ser consagrado. Pero, por supuesto, una vez consagrado su máxima propiedad es su capacidad de contribuir a la actividad santificante del mismo Cristo. Esta ambigüedad acerca del significado de 'esencial' surge cuando uno piensa en la función de una neurona en el cerebro humano. Por sí misma la neurona es 'esencialmente' un organismo unicelular. Pero al mismo tiempo está contribuyendo al pensamiento y al deseo humano en virtud de su esencia superior. Este caso, aunque en niveles diferentes, es bastante parecido al del pan eucarístico. El aspecto sobrenatural y milagroso de este último caso es que, por el poder del Espíritu, la realidad natural superior del pan brinca varios niveles de la jerarquía cósmica para llegar a la más alta de todas, el nivel de la Palabra encarnada.

La situación es muy similar a la del 'cuerpo místico' de Cristo. Cuando un converso es bautizado se vuelve parte de Cristo. Sin embargo él no cambia su esencia filosófica ordinaria. Él sigue siendo, en lo que a su esencia filosófica se refiere, un ser humano, pero un ser humano que está unido a Cristo en una forma real que solo puede ser descrita diciendo con San Pablo que ya no vive él, sino es Cristo que vive en él (Gal. 2,20). ¿Qué es más importante, su membresía en el cuerpo místico o su propia esencia filosófica? Yo creo que es más importante que él es parte de Cristo, y si hablamos de su naturaleza en el sentido más importante del término, él ya no existe como él mismo, sino más bien como parte de Cristo. Esto es semejante a lo que pasa en el mundo entero en el caso del 'existencial sobrenatural' de Rahner. Desde el mismo inicio la 'naturaleza' del mundo es una naturaleza sobrenatural a pesar del hecho de que todavía tiene una esencia filosófica que es meramente natural en sí misma.

¿Estará errado decir que la transubstanciación transforma el pan de la misa en Cristo mismo, pero al mismo tiempo el pan permanece pan? Yo no creo. No hay contradicción. No importa cuán milagrosa es la Eucaristía no hay contradicción en sostener que tiene dos 'esencias'. La segunda, esencia milagrosa se podría decir, desde un punto de vista, que es 'accidental' más que 'esencial'. Pero ese tipo de lenguaje es inadecuado, Nuestra forma ordinaria de hablar no es apta para expresar la naturaleza de la Eucaristía.

La recepción de la Eucaristía es un medio por el cual miembros humanos de Cristo son deificados. Sin perder su propia naturaleza se convierten en sus miembros. Cuando en el cielo los seres humanos se vuelvan perfectos, entonces serán tan puros y santos como el pan eucarístico ya lo es. La parusía será el tiempo en el que el universo entero se vuelva completamente sujeto a Cristo. En este tiempo la materia ordinaria está parcialmente bajo el control de seres humanos pecadores y de fuerzas demoníacas. Cuando el pecado haya terminado y los poderes malignos sean expulsados del mundo, entonces el universo mismo será plenamente el cuerpo cósmico de Cristo, sujeto enteramente a sus deseos y a la libertad de los hijos de Dios que son sus miembros. El cuerpo físico resucitado de Cristo ya está sujeto a él. El estado que ahora deseamos para nosotros es aquel en el cual el universo entero está sujeto de la misma manera, incluyendo nuestras propias naturalezas racionales y las entidades inferiores dentro de nosotros que ahora son parcialmente independientes de nuestras voluntades.

La doctrina de la Eucaristía era un obstáculo para la Iglesia del siglo XVI. Los Padres del Concilio no sabían nada acerca de moléculas o átomos, ni de la evidencia empírica que respalda su existencia dentro de los cuerpos humanos. Ellos simplemente usaban el mejor y más claro lenguaje que pudieron encontrar en su momento. Schillebeeckx estaba en lo correcto cuando decía que ellos simplemente repetían la doctrina que les habían dejado los Padres de la Iglesia en la mejor forma disponible para ellos, que era en términos de la transubstanciación tomista.

La teoría filosófica sugerida por Santo Tomás era buena para su momento, y aún era buena en el tiempo de Trento. Pero hoy, en vista de la moderna evidencia científica, parece inadecuada. La teoría de la jerarquía cósmica que yo propongo parece ser mejor. Muestra que mientras él estaba en la tierra el cuerpo físico de Cristo contenía en sí mismo partículas elementales, átomos, moléculas, etc., igual que los nuestros lo hacen. Cada una de esas entidades subordinadas tiene su propio acto de existencia. Pero en el momento de la consagración en la misa son sublimados por la realidad de Cristo, quien existe en los niveles racional y cósmico.

En el *Catecismo de la Iglesia Católica* (no. 1374) el Concilio de Trento es citado diciendo que '*la totalidad de Cristo es en verdad real y sustancialmente* contenida' en la Eucaristía. Luego cita la encíclica del Papa Pablo VI que nos dice que Trento quiere decir que la presencia de Jesús es real en el sentido más pleno posible: 'es una presencia sustancial por la cual ciertamente se hace presente Cristo, Dios y hombre, entero e íntegro' (*Mysterium Fidei*, no. 39). Este es el significado de sus palabras, 'en verdad, real y sustancialmente'. El Papa Pablo VI no era un físico. Él estaba simplemente repitiendo una doctrina que nos ha llegado de los Padres de la Iglesia, desde una época en la cual las moléculas y los átomos eran desconocidos.

¿Entonces cuál será el significado de las 'especies' del pan y el vino que Trento dice que permanecen después de la consagración en la misa? Tiene que ser la realidad del pan y el vino que ha sido sublimado por el Cristo cósmico como el símbolo real por el cual él alimenta espiritualmente los miembros de la Iglesia, su cuerpo místico.

III. El universo sacramental

Habiendo esquematizado una teoría moderna de transubstanciación ahora estamos en la posición de poder ver más claramente su relación con la transignificación. Podemos estar de acuerdo en un sentido cualificado con la afirmación de Schoonenberg de que 'la transubstanciación tiene lugar en una transignificación, una transfinalización'.[12] Cuando están consagradas las especies eucarísticas asumen un nuevo significado y un nuevo propósito en virtud del cual pueden funcionar como la causa simbólica de la unidad de la Iglesia y de la santificación del comulgante individual. Pero el significado que asumen es uno muy especial. Ahora significan no solo la unidad de la Iglesia sino también la real presencia local de Cristo, su disponibilidad aquí y ahora como un objeto de adoración y fuente de perdón, sanación y nueva vida en el Espíritu. No podrían en verdad poseer este significado si el Señor no estuviera realmente presente, si las especies eucarísticas no contuvieran ya lo que ellas significan. Ni podría la Iglesia ser una ni el creyente ser santificado en la manera poderosa que el símbolo pretende si ese no fuera el caso. La transubstanciación, eso es, la presencia real de Cristo mismo en las especies eucarísticas es lo que hace real a la transignificación y a la transfinalización.

Como el Papa Pablo VI insistió en su encíclica de 1965, *Mysterium Fidei,* hay peligro en usar el término transignificación si no se hace evidente su conexión con la transubstanciación. La Eucaristía no es solo una realidad simbólica, sino también cosmológica, algo que tiene que ver con el mundo temporal, espacial y material en el cual vivimos. Alguna filosofía moderna es incapaz de darle el peso debido a este aspecto cosmológico. Para eso necesitamos una cosmología que sintetice el punto de vista subjetivo no solo con el más objetivo y empírico de la ciencia, sino también con la doctrina tradicional de la Iglesia.

'El lenguaje de la transubstanciación . . . subraya el hecho de que la totalidad de la creación es en último término sacramental, que ella tiene, en el orden que Dios le ha dado, la capacidad de encarnar la acción en la que Dios da su vida al hombre' (Powers, 185–86). Porque la materia es por naturaleza una realidad potencialmente sacramental, el poder de encarnarse a sí mismo poseído por el Logos puede alcanzar más allá de su inmediato cuerpo personal para transformar el pan y el vino eucarístico, y a través de esto la comunidad que rinde culto. Al final este poder eventualmente transformará el mundo entero. Así, en su epístola a los romanos, San Pablo habla de como la 'creación misma será librada de la esclavitud de la corrupción para entrar a la libertad gloriosa de los hijos de Dios. Sabemos que toda la creación ha estado gimiendo con dolores de parto hasta ahora. Y no solo la creación sino también nosotros, que tenemos las primicias del Espíritu, gemimos dentro de nosotros mismos aguardando la adopción como hijos, la redención de nuestro cuerpo' (Rom 8, 21.23). La transformación de la creación, que ha tenido lugar parcialmente en algunas personas, envolverá el mundo a lo último. Como cuerpo cósmico del Logos mismo recibirá el poder transformante de su resurrección y se convertirá, si no parte del 'cuerpo místico' en estricto sentido, al menos tan asociado con él que compartirá en 'la gloria de los hijos de Dios'. La señal y promesa de esta transformación final escatológica es la transformación del pan y del vino eucarístico.

Nadie ha expresado esto en forma más bella que Teilhard de Chardin en varios de sus ensayos cortos. En *La Misa sobre el Mundo* invitaba al Señor a darle poder para pronunciar sobre la creación las palabras transformantes 'Este es mi cuerpo . . . Esta es mi sangre'.[13] En otro ensayo describe la experiencia de un 'amigo' no identificado, probablemente él mismo, quien de rodillas frente al santísimo sacramento, experimentó una impresión muy extraña' (op. cit., 47). Mientras él velaba y rezaba, la hostia en la custodia frente a él gradualmente empezó a expandir sus límites hasta que cubrió todo el mundo, tomando dentro de sí, en la medida posible, la sustancia de todas las cosas.

Teilhard parece habernos transmitido una intuición que se le había confiado para nuestra era científica. El universo, que los científicos analizan y cuya estructura han esclarecido, en diversas formas, hasta un extremo nunca soñado en épocas anteriores, es entendido de la manera más profunda en términos de la Eucaristía. Es realmente el cuerpo cósmico de Cristo, una realidad destinada a ser glorificada por ser 'eucaristizada' o 'transubstanciada'. Por tanto la historia del universo es una especie de

Eucaristía, una liturgia cósmica. La materia para ser ofrecida fue preparada en la creación y entregada a las creaturas, como los sacerdotes de la creación, para que fuera ofrecida al Padre. Por causa del pecado el ofrecimiento no se hizo, hasta que finalmente en la plenitud de los tiempos el verdadero sumo sacerdote vino y 'entró una vez para siempre en el lugar santísimo logrando así eterna redención, ya no mediante sangre de machos cabríos ni de becerros sino mediante su propia sangre.' (Heb. 9,12). Por y en el sacrificio de Jesústodo el universo material-espiritual ha sido ofrecido y transformado parcialmente. Hasta ahora el poder transformador de este sacrificio no ha completado su trabajo, porque nosotros no hemos completado aun nuestra ratificación de la ofrenda. Pero esperamos la venida del día en que nuestra ofrenda sea completa y él, a quien ella se ofrece, hará nuevas todas las cosas (Ap. 21,5). Se hará nuevo en Jesús pues su realidad más profunda consiste en que es su cuerpo cósmico el que en definitiva compartirá su glorificación personal.

En el momento presente la crisis ecológica exige de nosotros un énfasis especial en el aspecto cósmico del simbolismo eucarístico. Sabiendo que la tierra y el universo encuentran su unidad y realidad más profunda en Cristo, tenemos que aprender a respetar su integridad y tratar de convertirnos en custodios y sacerdotes y no en explotadores de la creación. Comiendo del pan eucarístico fortalecemos nuestro sentido de dependencia del mundo y nuestra unidad con él. Es un símbolo sacramental de Cristo compartiendo su vida con nosotros, lo cual merece nuestra reverencia profunda.

Esta comprensión nos permite poner nuestros conocimientos científicos del mundo en perspectiva. La ciencia es un maravilloso regalo de Dios, pero no cumplirá el propósito para el que Dios nos la dio hasta que no sea elevada a la sabiduría superior que sólo nuestro ofrecimiento de 'la misa en el mundo' nos proporciona. A medida que nuestra civilización planetaria emergente aprende a ofrecer esta misa, la dureza reduccionista, debida a la exclusiva atención a los mecanismos del mundo, irá disminuyendo y nos iremos abriendo a una actitud más humana.

Esto se reflejará en nuestra comprensión del sentido o propósito de la tecnología, gemela de la ciencia, y de las otras técnicas modernas que extienden el espíritu de la tecnología a la vida social y económica de nuestra raza. La construcción y el uso de mecanismos serán vistos como ordenados a la totalidad integrada de la existencia humana y de toda la creación en el Logos, como un servicio invalorable concedido a metas y esfuerzos que exceden por lejos la esfera de lo meramente tecnológico. El mito de la máquina, la glorificación de los mecanismos por sí mismos dará paso a un ideal de servicio y adoración, de *opus Dei* cósmico, en el cual las técnicas materiales, sociales y económicas apoyan y facilitan la aspiración espiritual y la gloria divina.

Translated by María Isabel Reyna Calvani, Caracas, Venezuela

Notas

1. J. Neuner and J. Dupuis, eds., *The Christian Faith,* rev. ed. (New York: Alba House, 1982), no. 1527.

2. Edward Schillebeeckx, *The Eucharist* [= E] (London: Sheed & Ward, 1968), 54.

3. Piet Schoonenberg, "Transubstantiation" [= T], *Concilium* 24 (1967): 78–91, en 83.

4. William B. Ashworth Jr., "Catholicism and Early Modern Science," en *God and Nature,* ed. David C. Lindberg y Ronald L. Numbers (Berkeley: University of California Press, 1986), cap. 5, en 151. También Frederick Copleston, *A History of Philosophy,* 9 vols. (New York: Doubleday, 1985), 4:126–28.

5. Joseph M. Powers, *Eucharistic Theology* (New York: Herder & Herder, 1967), 166.

6. Robert J. Russell, William R. Stoeger, y George V. Coyne, eds., *Physics, Philosophy, and Theology* (Vatican City: Vatican Observatory, 1988 [distribuido, excepto en Italia y Ciudad del Vaticano, por Univ. of Notre Dame Press]), M1–M14.

7. Col. 1:15–20; Eph. 1:9–10, 20–23; y Rom. 8:19–23. Junto con estos, John 1:1–5 y Heb. 1:3–4, así como 1 Cor. 8:6 y Phil. 2:6–11, tienen un significado cósmico semejante.

8. David Noel Freedman, ed., *The Anchor Bible Dictionary,* 6 vols. (New York: Doubleday, 1992), 1:771.

9. Ernst Mayr, *This Is Biology: The Science of the Living World* (Cambridge,

MA: Belknap Press of Harvard University Press, 1997), 19, citando a François Jacob, *The Logic of Life: A History of Heredity* (New York: Pantheon, 1973), 302.

10. Michael Polanyi, *The Tacit Dimension* (Garden City, NY: Doubleday-Anchor, 1967), 35–36. Por supuesto la analogía de Polanyi no prueba sino más bien ilustra su punto de vista.

11. Bernard Lonergan, *Method in Theology* (New York: Herder & Herder, 1972), 241.

12. Powers, *Eucharistic Theology*, 173.

13. Pierre Teilhard de Chardin, *Hymn of the Universe,* trad. Gerald Vann (New York: Harper Torchbooks, 1965), 19–37, esp. 23.

A NEW MEANING
OF CHRISTIAN WORSHIP

And so we can now say that the goal of worship and the goal of creation as a whole are one and the same—divinization, a world of freedom and love. But this means that the historical makes its appearance in the cosmic. The cosmos is not a kind of closed building, a stationary container in which history may by chance take place. It is itself movement, from its one beginning to its one end. In a sense, creation is history.

This can be understood in several ways. For example, against the background of the modern evolutionary worldview, Teilhard de Chardin depicted the cosmos as a process of ascent, a series of unions. From very simple beginnings the path leads to ever greater and more complex unities, in which multiplicity is not abolished but merged into a growing synthesis, leading to the "Noosphere" in which spirit and its understanding embrace the whole and are blended into a kind of living organism. Invoking the epistles to the Ephesians and Colossians, Teilhard looks on Christ as the energy that strives toward the Noosphere and finally incorporates everything in its "fullness."

From here Teilhard went on to give a new meaning to Christian worship: the transubstantiated host is the anticipation of the transformation and divinization of matter in the christological "fullness." In his view, the Eucharist provides the movement of the cosmos with its direction; it anticipates its goal and at the same time urges it on.

Pope Benedict XVI (Joseph Ratzinger)
The Spirit of the Liturgy

ABOUT THE AUTHOR

Richard J. Pendergast (1927–2012) was a Jesuit priest with a doctorate in physics and licentiates in philosophy and theology, who devoted his life to seeking the integration of modern science and divine revelation. His aim was to update the Christian synthesis of St. Thomas Aquinas, based on the medieval static worldview, to reflect evolution, the view of cosmic reality as dynamic process. A scholar of first rank whose research appeared in peer-reviewed professional journals, he yet preferred pastoral ministry to academic life. He deeply desired to address the general public, believers as well as nonbelievers, to offer insight into problems that may disturb the faith of the former or impede the latter's search for God. He wrote five books over thirty years, and these manuscripts are now being published in a series of five volumes, complemented by Volume 6, a trilingual reprint of his study on the teaching of the Catholic Church concerning the real presence of Christ in the Eucharist. Richard Pendergast was a seminal thinker, whose work presents a bold Christian vision—a living universe of meaning and hope.

A CHRISTIAN COSMOLOGY

The Catholic Church does not have a formal teaching on evolution at this time. But people wonder about the meaning of their lives as experienced in their own culture, which today is dominated by science. Charles Darwin's theory of evolution has raised many questions and led to diverse claims. In this work addressed to the general reader, the author discusses what has been reliably established by science, distinguishing it from interpretations of the theory guided by philosophical assumptions. Seeking a coherent picture of the world, Richard Pendergast integrates scientific knowledge with what we have in Sacred Scripture and lays the foundation of a Christian cosmology. It is the beginning of a venture for generations.

ABOUT THE EDITOR

A native of Budapest, Hungary, Valerie Miké obtained a liberal arts degree at Manhattanville College, worked at Bell Labs in systems engineering, and earned a doctorate in mathematics at the Courant Institute of New York University. She went on to participate in the introduction of mathematical techniques in medicine and pursued graduate studies in ethics and the philosophy of science. She is professor emerita of biostatistics at Weill Medical College of Cornell University and former head of the biostatistics department at the Sloan-Kettering Institute for Cancer Research. Her study of ethical issues pertaining to uncertainty in biomedical science and technology led to the notion of an "ethics of evidence"—an approach to uncertainty widely applicable to decision-making in human affairs. She has established the Ethics of Evidence Foundation, with a mission that includes publishing the work of scholars in related fields.

The motto of
The Ethics of Evidence Foundation, Inc.

**All our dignity consists in thought. . . .
Let us then strive to think well;
that is the basic principle of morality.**

Blaise Pascal